D0909711

A BAR CROSS LIAR

A BAR CROSS LIAR

BIBLIOGRAPHY OF EUGENE MANLOVE RHODES WHO
LOVED THE WEST-THAT-WAS WHEN HE WAS YOUNG

by W. H. HUTCHINSON

REDLANDS PRESS, STILLWATER, OKLAHOMA, 1959

637218

REFERENCE ROOM

Z
8741
H91 B

Library of Congress Catalog Card Number: 60-17854

Copyright 1959 by W. H. Hutchinson

Published by

Redlands Press, Stillwater, Okla.

A

FOR:

Leslie E. Bliss
and
J. Frank Dobie

Who shortened the trail by the songs they knew.

PREFACE

This wayward gathering has been prepared for the lovers and collectors of Eugene Manlove Rhodes and his works. That it may appeal to them is a desideratum devoutly to be wished.

There are many reasons, in one man's mind at least, for the labor, the time and the hazard that have brought this Bibliography to pass. The very best of these reasons is now set forth.

In early 1931, Retta [*Mrs. Stanwood*] Badger, a friend of Rhodes from his stay in Los Angeles in the 1920s, was preparing an article about him for the *Los Angeles Times*. Before submitting her final piece, she sent Rhodes her keynote for his reaction:

"*The cowboy, with a sound psychology, made pride the ally of achievement and not enemy. He was too proud to give up, too proud to be outdone, to weaken, to yield or to boast; too proud to alibi, too proud to allow the strong man to oppress him or to impose upon the weak.*"

In reply, [*May 29, 1931*] Rhodes summated his lifelong feelings: "You have touched upon the very point. The *star system* has never obtained on the Free Range. Better way to state it is 'in open country' for the same code was held by miners and merchants. No superlatives! 'He's a good man' 'He'll do to take along'. That was the highest praise.

"You have met Bob Martin! Well — Bob Martin, Cole Railston, Pres Lewis, Frank Bojorquez, Felipe Lucero, Hiram Yoast, Johnny Dines, Emil James, Pete Johnson, Lon Roberts, Tom Ross — *any* 'sclusively *old time cowboy* — was just as good a man as Ed Borein, Charlie Russell, Will Rogers, Gene Rhodes or Will James. These last five would hope and expect and deserve to be received as *equals* by the first bunch — but no man ever lived they would recognize as the best. The best in some one line — Certainly! But when these lads said *a good man* — they meant a man who would do his damndest every time. More particularly, they meant by a good man the man who would help you out of trouble, sickness, danger, debt, disgrace or damnation. Their way of putting it was: 'I'd be glad to see Bob Martin saunterin' along when I was in a tight'. Meaning, in a tight place — but they never said more than tight.

IX

"That is what I have zealously tried to put in my stories. 'Good Men' — never a hero. Good MEN and TRUE. Bransford and Mc-Gregor *and* Pringle — Johnny Dines and Charlie See and *Jerome* Martin, and Pete Henderson and Judge Hinkle *and* George Scarborough — every one just as good as any other one.

"People say, 'Yes, Mr. Rhodes — your story people are amusing but you dreamed them. They never happened.' I didn't dream them. They were twice as interesting in the flesh than my poor report ever was. Twice as witty. And they went through more hazardous adventures practically every month of every year than those I have set to paper. There is a reason — When they got wind of an adventure roundabout *they went to look-see.* Whereas most of us, at any hint of adventure, lock the door and telephone to the police.

"And so on and on and on. But if — if you want to please me — this is the line to take. Just bear in mind that Will Rogers, and we know he would be a good man in any company and any place, *just passed as one of the boys* and excited no remark. So of the others, if all of them went to a round-up tomorrow and did their work well, this would excite no remark. That was what was expected of them. That was what they were there for."

We are well past the century mark in the development of our own truly native art form in prose — the "Western" — horse opera in all its mutants. It would seem that its early frontier-Gothic period has become crystalline in the spate of offerings that overload the coaxial cables, microwave relays and video tape machines these parlous times. For these offerings from the bat cave called television we need an antidote and we need it badly. 'Gene Rhodes, in any way, shape or form, is a part of that antidote and is a most vital part of our literary heritage from the West-That-Was.

Most of my acknowledgements are made in the text hereafter. I must make especial mention of help from the Henry E. Huntington Library in providing from Rockefeller Funds a grant-in-aid that made initial work hereon possible.

W. H. Hutchinson

Chico, California
2-XII-1958

x

CONTENTS

BRIEF BAEDEKER

Vincent Starrett compiled the first check-list of Rhodes in THE HIRED MAN ON HORSEBACK. Frank V. Dearing, Jeff C. Dykes and W. H. Hutchinson, working separately and then in combination, materially expanded and corrected this initial offering for inclusion in THE LITTLE WORLD WADDIES. A further refinement appeared in A BAR CROSS MAN.

In preparing this true Bibliography, the author has had the continued generous assistance of Jeff Dykes plus innumerable courtesies from Mr. Graham Watson, Curtis Brown Ltd., London, and Mr. H. F. Juergens, Grossett & Dunlap, New York. Invaluable data has come from Mr. Paul Brooks, Houghton Mifflin Co., and Mr. Erd Brandt of the *Saturday Evening Post*. Assistance beyond the call of courtesy or friendship has come from Miss Mary Isabel Fry, Huntington Library; from Mr. Michael Harrison, Sacramento, Calif.; and Benjamin Kirby, Esq., of Los Angeles. Sins of omission and commission belong properly to none of these.

Contrary to usual practice, Rhodes' books have been listed and discussed *after* his magazine appearances simply because his books are but his magazine stories with very minor revisions. In but one book, WEST IS WEST, is there an appreciable body of previously unpublished material.

The magazine stories have been arranged *chronologically herein to show Rhodes' progress up the commercial ladder and to show the great gaps in his remunerative productivity*. Lest there be any misapprehension, Rhodes wrote for money, even as the rest of us, and the fact that he created more lasting wares than the coin he received is not unknown in the trade. Those who insist upon having his stories arranged by publication may purchase A BAR CROSS MAN and bring the check list therein up-to-date.

It will be noted that Rhodes used the same title in several instances for stories in different magazines. He carefully selected his titles to fit his story content, or his personal intent contained in that story. That he had used a title before was no bar to its re-use when another story warranted or demanded this same title.

Much of Rhodes work has appeared in posthumous collections. For brevity's sake, these appearances have been symbolized thus:

H — THE HIRED MAN ON HORSEBACK
W — THE LITTLE WORLD WADDIES
O — THE BEST NOVELS AND STORIES OF EUGENE MANLOVE RHODES
R — THE RHODES READER

By comparing the publication dates of these works with the other reprint data given, the interested may determine the first appearances in book form. For the benefit of *aficionados* and to show how an author's own opinions may differ from those of his later admirers, the pieces that Rhodes selected for inclusion in the proposed [1932] BAR CROSS EDITION of his works have been symboilzed thus: †

The letters NW appearing after a story type indicate that it was not a "western" in the accepted sense even though the story may have had a geographically western locale.

The lack of annotations for certain of the magazine stories indicates that they either have been discussed fully elsewhere or that no comment seemed warranted. Wherever possible, the amount received by Rhodes for his offerings has been shown after the name of the purchasing magazine.

Buen Provecho!

A BAR CROSS LIAR

MAGAZINE APPEARANCES

CHARLEY GRAHAM. *Land of Sunshine* (later *Out West*), April, 1896. W, Verse.

See Keleher's THE FABULOUS FRONTIER and A BAR CROSS MAN, this author, for data on Charles Graham.

THE WHITE MAN'S BURDEN. *Oakland,* [*Calif.*] *Saturday Night,* June 10, 1899. Verse.

Biting rejoinder to Kipling's poem of the same title, *McClure's,* February, 1899, which had been reprinted in this feminist newspaper, 2/25/1899.

A BLOSSOM OF BARREN LANDS. *Land of Sunshine,* October, 1899. H, W, Verse.

Eulogy of the yucca; reprinted *New Mexico Historical Review,* April, 1935.

A BALLADE OF GRAY HILLS. *Land of Sunshine,* November, 1900. W, Verse.

TE DEUM LAUDAMUS. *Land of Sunshine,* January, 1901. W, Verse.

Denunciation of United States for Imperialism in the Philippines. As "Io Paean! Io Paean!" had appeared in unidentified newspaper, 11/16/1900.

AS IS THE NEEDLE TO THE POLE. *New Orleans Times-Democrat,* March 24, 1901. W, Verse.

THE PROFESSOR'S EXPERIMENT. *Munsey's Argosy,* December, 1901. Fiction.

Norman Metcalf, Berkeley, Calif., has found mention of this story. Neither he nor I have seen it. Probably the FIRST fiction.

THE HOUR AND THE MAN. *Out West* (later *Sunset*), $10.00, January, 1902. Fiction.

Godawful frontier-Gothic. Can be used as route map for horseback travel from White Oaks to Lake Valley via San Augustin Pass, New Mexico.

LUBLY GE-GE AND GRUFFANGRIM. *Out West,* February, 1902. Fiction.

First appearance of Rhodes favorite hero-type — the man outside the legalities but all man.

A BALLADE OF WILD BEES. *Out West,* March, 1902. W, Verse.

Inspired by Sharlot M. Hall, a fellow contributor to *Out West* at this time.

THE CAPTAIN OF THE GATE. *Out West,* April, 1902. W, (poem), Fiction.

Contained the poem, "With an Evening Primrose". Based upon the killing of Felix Knox, gambler, by Apache near the Yorke Ranch between Lordsburg, N.M., and Clifton, Arizona.

THE BAR CROSS LIAR. *Out West,* June, 1902. Fiction.

Rhodes' first use of himself as a major contributor to the story protagonist.

THE DESIRE OF THE MOTH. *Out West,* October, 1902. Fiction.

As expanded, makes pp. 213/219 and 272/273 in WEST IS WEST: see, also, *"Sons of the Soil."*

HIS FATHER'S FLAG. *McClure's,* $40.00, October, 1902. Fiction: NW.

Until discovery of the *Argosy* piece of December, 1901, this was believed to be Rhodes' first Eastern appearance. Involves a Confederate flag and scion in the Boxer Rebellion for the first venture beyond known bounds. When J. B. O'Neil was promoting the *Bar Cross Edition* in 1932, Rhodes wrote him as follows: "This is pretty dreadful. If you are so ill-advised as to use it — I'll have to make changes. It is too high school."

THE WHITE FLYER. *Munsey's Argosy,* December, 1902. Fiction.

Outlaw-railroad story with a touch of wry. Michael Harrison sent me a veritable copy of this yarn.

LOVED I NOT HONOR MORE. *Out West,* February, 1903. R, Fiction.

Rhodes' personal refusal to sell horses to England during the Boer War.

SLAVES OF THE RING. *Out West,* June, 1903. Fiction.

Rhodes' college associates and fraternity in a New Mexico setting. The basic mechanics of the poker game in this story were later used in "Over, Under, Around and Through" and in "Once in the Saddle".

THE BLUNDERER'S MARK. *Out West,* November, 1903. Fiction.

Virtually the same story as "The Captain of the Gate", April, 1902, but in a Wyoming setting. Henry Wallace Phillips appears as a character in this yarn which is based upon Nate Champion's lone fight to the death in The Johnson County War.

A TOUCH OF NATURE. *McClure's,* January, 1905. Fiction.

H. W. Phillips had sole credit for this story which is unmistakably Rhodesian in origin. N. Howard "Jack" Thorp tells the same story as fact in PARDNER OF THE WIND, pp. 220/221. Reprinted, RED SAUNDER'S PETS AND OTHER CRITTERS, with Phillips still as sole author. This lack of recognition, as well as cash, seems to have been the price paid by Rhodes for Phillips' assistance.

SONS OF THE SOIL. *Out West,* November, 1905. Fiction.

Conclusion to "Desire of the Moth", October, 1902; the gap cannot be explained unless it be that C. F. Lummis chopped the original into two reasonably self-contained components and delayed use of the second.

SEALED ORDERS. *Out West,* July, 1906. Fiction: NW.

ON VELVET. *All Story* (Bob Davis, the famous editor, paid $175.00 for the first four stories that appeared herein), September, 1906. Fiction.

Rhodes created one of his own legends with this story. A duded-up youth, returning to New Mexico from college in California, borrows a horse to ride from the railroad to his ranch home. The boys, naturally, give him an outlaw and the seeming dude, naturally, rides him slick and pretty. This story has been told so often in New Mexico that it has the effect of fact. Two men who rode the *Jornada* with Rhodes, Bob Martin and Carroll McCombs, have classed both this story and the outgrowth legend as pure fiction.

AN INTERLUDE. *All Story,* October, 1906. Fiction: NW

Based on Rhodes' experiences during summer vacation from University of the Pacific, 1899, this contains much Californiana of the Monterey/Carmel area. Marks the first usage by Rhodes of a young Easterner as an expository audience for Rhodes' West and is the first indication in print of Rhodes' resentment over the Easterner feeling that all Westerners were tawny barbarians.

STICKY PIERCE, DIPLOMAT. *Out West,* October, 1906. †, R, Fiction.

More on Rhodes *vs* prevailing Easterner attitudes towards the West and its people; bronco *vs* broncho gets much attention.

A PINK TRIP SLIP. *Out West,* January, 1907. Fiction: NW.

Based on Rhodes' experiences during the train trip East in 1906 that began his exile from New Mexico.

NEIGHBORS. *All Story,* February, 1907. Fiction.

The central character in this story is Pat Coghlan, one-time King of Tularosa and fence for Billy the Kid's stolen cattle. It seems that this makes a fair picture of Pat's disintegration after his downfall.

WILDCAT REPRESENTS. *All Story,* March, 1907. Fiction.

Political cleavage between Democrats and Republicans in Las Cruces during the 1890s with attendant personal animosities and allegiances. The use of rattlesnakes to foil a lynch mob in this story was repeated in "Stepsons of Light". Reprinted, unidentified Western pulp magazine, pp. 67/80, about 1927.

THE NUMISMATIST. *Satevepost,* 3/2/1907. †, R, Fiction.

Signed collaboration with H. W. Phillips; based upon the Cleveland/Blaine presidential contest when Sig Lindauer and other Deming-ites sent Watt Wilkerson to Silver City to trap the denizens thereof into election bets. Reprinted, TROLLEY FOLLY, Bobbs Merrill, 1909, a collection of Phillips' short stories, without credit to Rhodes. This omission was not due to Bobbs Merrill but to a misunderstanding of the properties by Mrs. Phillips who handled the matter during her husband's illness. Reprint of this book by New York Book Company, 1913.

THE PUNISHMENT AND THE CRIME. *Satevepost,* 4/20/- 1907. †, Fiction.

Another collaboration with Phillips. Same reprint data as given above in TROLLEY FOLLY. This makes a veritable Baedeker to the cow outfits that used Engle, N. M., as shipping and supply center in the 1890s. Rhodes swore it was "2/3rds truth" but Carroll McCombs, then wagon boss for the Bar Cross, does not remember the incident of cow-camp, kangaroo-court justice it purports to relate.

RULE O' THUMB. *Out West,* June, 1907. Fiction: NW.

An account of a Rhodesian experience while teaching school at Alto, New Mexico. The problem to be solved by arithmetic was to fence a perfectly square horse-pasture with a three-wire fence, posts twelve feet apart. Posts cost 1c each; a spool of wire, 440 yards long, cost $3.30 with staples thrown in. The fence was to cost exactly 3 1/3c per acre. How many acres did the pasture contain and what were its dimensions?

EXTRA NUMBER. *Satevepost,* 6/1/1907. Fiction: NW.

THE END OF A STORY. *Out West,* July, 1907. Fiction: NW.

Based upon the death of Mrs. S. I. Rooke, telephone operator at Folsom, N. M., who warned forty families of an impending flood and was found, thereafter, twelve miles down-cañon with her head-set still clamped in place.

THE LINE OF LEAST RESISTANCE. *Out West*, August, 1907. Fiction.

Descriptive matter in this story makes most of Chap. XVI, "The Little Eohippus," being pp. 205/212 in BRANSFORD IN ARCADIA. This portion was unchanged in both serial and book versions. It was the Gonzalez ranch on the Rio Grande above Engle Ferry which is recalled nostalgically in "No Mean City."

THE LONG SHIFT. *McClure's*, $250.00, August, 1907. R, Fiction.

Hard-rock mining story, making pp. 43/53 in WEST IS WEST with addition last 11 lines, p. 53. Reprinted WESTERN ROUNDUP, Bantam Book No. 756, and used in their United Kingdom and Empire edition of this volume.

A BEGGAR ON HORSEBACK. *Out West*, November, 1907. Fiction.

Jeff Bransford *vs* Easterners in a train wreck.

THE COME ON. *Satevepost*, $600.00, 11/23-30/1907. †, Fiction.

Opening section reprinted, THE AMERICAN WEST, World, Cleveland and New York, 1946. Eugene Cunningham prepared the manuscript for this reprint, changing a few words in the process and chopping it off at about 3,100 words where, as a single short story, it had to end. See Book List under THE DESIRE OF THE MOTH.

THE AWAITED HOUR. *Everybody's*, $114.00, May, 1908. †, Fiction: NW.

Unjustly convicted husband escapes from Eastern penitentiary to gain his revenge. Rhodes was working on this story as early as May, 1902 while still living in New Mexico; his plot germ coming from David and Bathsheba.

A TOUCH OF NATURE. *Out West*, July, 1908. †, Ficton.

Situation comedy using young Easterner in New Mexico; marks first appearance of "John Wesley Pringle." Portions make pp. 238/239 in WEST IS WEST.

THE TORCH. *Out West*, August, 1908. †, Fiction: NW.

Another story from Rhodes' college days.

THE GOD FROM THE MACHINE. *Redbook*, $100.00, October, 1908. Fiction: NW.

Summer romance in New York state setting.

CHECK. *Satevepost*, 10/3/1908. †, Fiction.

Signed collaboration with Henry W. Phillips, using aspects of the Rhodes/Ritch feud from Rhodes' side of the argument.

THE ENCHANTED VALLEY. *Redbook,* March, 1909. R, Fiction.

Makes pp. 274/286, WEST IS WEST; reprinted, *Zane Grey's Western Magazine,* March-April, 1947. A version of the basic story herein was used by Arthur Brisbane in his column, early in 1933, which moved Rhodes to wry comment.

A NEIGHBOR. *Satevepost,* 3/6/1909. †, Fiction.

AN EXECUTIVE MIND. *Satevepost,* 4/24/1909. †, Fiction.

Makes Prologue chapter, "The Little Eohippus," being pp. 1/26, BRANSFORD IN ARCADIA. Another aspect of the Rhodes/Ritch feud, virtually from life.

BELL THE CAT. *Pacific Monthly* (later *Sunset*), $60.00, May, 1909. Fiction.

Makes pp. 126/144, WEST IS WEST, with padding; book version reprinted *Zane Grey's Western Magazine,* December, 1947.

THE MAN WITH A COUNTRY. *Satevepost,* 7/3/1909.†,Fiction.

Expatriates from many lands stage a Fourth of July celebration in Baja California. This is as blatant as Rhodes ever became on the inner fire of his love of country; it is too obvious to have warranted reprinting.

This was Rhodes' first independent submission to *Satevepost;* first rejected by them in 1907, he rewrote it in six different versions and lengths before they bought it. Rupert Hughes told this bibliographer that when the *Post* first received the manuscript, they thought H. W. Phillips was using a pseudonym, the handwriting of the two men being so equally illegible.

THE FOOL'S HEART. *All Story,* Sept., 1909. Fiction.

Based upon an actual New Mexico happening of two men each being convicted and hanged for the crime committed by the other; circumstantial evidence the cause.
Makes pp. 145/168, WEST IS WEST; reprinted, *Pocket Book of Mystery Stories,* 1941.

THE STAR OF EMPIRE. *Satevepost,* 9/4/1909. †, Fiction.

Reprinted, *Best Stories from the Southwest,* Hilton R. Greer; Dallas, 1928; excerpt reprinted, *America in the Southwest,* Pearce and Hendon; Albuquerque, 1933.

THE TROUBLE MAN. *Satevepost,* 11/20/1909. †, R, Fiction.

Probably based upon the Lee/Good, sometimes called Good/Cooper, range troubles. Jeff Bransford sings "The Little Eohippus" for the first time herein.

GOOD MEN AND TRUE. *Satevepost,* 1/8-15/1910. O (Book version) Fiction.

See Book List for data.

LEX TALIONIS. *Pacific Monthly,* $50.00, Feb., 1910. NW, Fiction.
This is the last purely frontier-Gothic effusion. Data in the Fred Lockley Collection, Huntington Library, shows that this story was received by the magazine in November, 1909; it is the assumption here that this was an early and unsold effort which Rhodes finally disposed of for small return.

THE LINE OF LEAST RESISTANCE. *Satevepost,* 8/13-9/3/-1910. W (poem only) Fiction.
See Booklets for data; contained the poem "White Fingers" which appeared, also, in an unidentified newspaper as "She Plays Upon Her Mandolin."

GOOD MEN AND TRUE. See Book List for, 8/26/1910.

BINGHAMPTON [N.Y.] PRESS AND REPUBLICAN 1910/1914
During these years, Rhodes contributed various verses, opinions and the like to the column conducted by Jules Livingston in both these papers. Rhodes signed himself either *Etaoin* or *Qwert Yuiop.*

THE HOUSE THAT JACK BUILT. *Satevepost,* $200.00, 4/1/-1911. Essay.
Humorous blast at Frank Harris Hitchcock, then Taft's Postmaster-General, for trying to raise the postal rates on printed matter.

A NUMBER OF THINGS. *Satevepost,* 4/8/1911. †, R, Fiction.
Situation comedy of Socorro county politics and personalities.

SAY NOW SHIBBOLETH. *Satevepost,* 4/22/1911. O, Essay.
See Booklets; reprinted, *Present Day Essays,* Holt, New York, 1923, pp. 236/261, with critical discussion of same, pp. 245/346; this phrase used by Bernard DeVoto for a section heading in his *The Literary Fallacy,* Boston, 1944.

THE BARRED DOOR. *Satevepost,* 5/6/1911. H (excerpt) R, Essay.
Biting denunciation of all concerned with the consistent denial of statehood to New Mexico. A. B. Fall furnished much of the material used by Rhodes, who submitted his piece with the title "Stung" only to have the *Post* change it to a less blunt instrument.

THE PRINCE OF TONIGHT. *Satevepost,* 10/19/1912. † H, (excerpt) NW, Fiction.
Idealized depiction of Rhodes' trip east with a cattle train to meet and marry May Davison.

THE LITTLE EOHIPPUS. *Satevepost,* 11/30-12/26/1912. O, (Book version), Fiction.
See Book List for BRANSFORD IN ARCADIA.
In *Songs of Horses,* Cambridge, 1920, Robert Frothingham uses a couplet

about "The Little Eohippus;" in his Notes to *A Texas Cowboy*, New York, 1950, J. Frank Dobie quotes a long anecdote from this story.

Rhodes had started work on this story late in 1908, making a long gestation period.

OF THE LOST LEGION. *Everybody's*, April, 1913. †, NW, Fiction.

Signed collaboration with Lawrence Yates, newspaperman of Owego, New York.

SEALED ORDERS. *Satevepost*, $400.00, 5/10/1913. Fiction.

Makes pp. 169/190, WEST IS WEST.

The heroine, facing a Fate Worse Than Death in an El Paso brothel, is saved by a hero from outside the law. One of two instances where Rhodes even hinted at unsanctified sex and the only case where he admitted that there was sexual immorality for money.

REVERSION TO TYPE. *Sunset*, June, 1913. Fiction.

A Westerner, grown rich and pompous, is redeemed by reverting to the code of his raising.

CONSIDER THE LIZARD. *Satetvepost*, $500.00, 6/28/1913. O, Fiction.

Reprinted, *The Saturday Evening Post Treasury*, New York, 1954; sold to Warner Brothers, 1958, for use in the television series, *Colt 45*.

A RAGTIME LADY. *Satevepost*, 7/26/1913. †, NW, Fiction.

Signed collaboration with Lawrence Yates, being romance in a New York state setting.

Reprinted, *Today's Short Stories Analyzed*, New York, 1918; Robert Wilson Neal did a most adequate dissection of the story to show the novice how the whole was made. Not so much a critique as a session in vocational guidance.

BRANSFORD IN ARCADIA. See Book List for, 1/23/1914.

BEYOND THE DESERT. *McClure's*, Feb., 1914. O, (Book version), Fiction.

When Rhodes altered "Good Men and True" for book publication, one change was to save "Sandy McGregor" for future use which here is made. This is the other hint at unsanctified sex in all of Rhodes' stories and is the only suggested seduction on his record.

Makes pp. 11/42, WEST IS WEST, with addition of 3,500 words of padding. This has been the reprinted version with the exception of the *Prologue* portion.

Reprinted, *Great Tales of the American West*, New York, 1945; also in *Out West*, Boston, 1955: as "The Hand of the Potter", Rhodes' personal title, distributed by Metropolitan Newspaper Syndicate, 1923.

WHEN THE BILLS COME IN. *Harper's Weekly,* 6/13/1914. Essay.

See Booklets under *Say Now Shibboleth.*

HIT THE LINE HARD. *Satevepost,* 3/27-4/3/1915. †, O, Fiction.

See Book List under THE DESIRE OF THE MOTH.

This title may be familiar to an older generation as a part of Teddy Roosevelt's classic adjuration: "Don't flinch, don't foul, hit the line hard!"

THE FOOL'S HEART. *Satevepost,* 5/1/1915. R, Fiction.

The tightest plotting Rhodes ever did; very hard to fault it in any way. Adapted into a two-act play, 1919, by Milton Charles Newcomb and produced by him at Ohio Wesleyan University with his students as the cast. Reprinted, *Suspense Stories,* Dellbook 367, New York, 1950; adapted for television by Ruth Woodman and performed on the CBS network program, "Suspense," 1/16/1951.

LITTLE NEXT DOOR. *Out West,* Jan., 1916. W, Verse.

Interesting because the first draft was written at Lewis Fort's house in Roswell, N.M., in 1905.

Portions used in "The Desire of the Moth" for which see 2/26/1916.

HOW THE DREAMS CAME TRUE. *Out West,* Feb., 1916. Essay.

Disjointed, subjective venture into the early exploration of the Far West that is pretty awful. A supposition is that Rhodes sold this to *Out West* at a much earlier date and that it was not used until the magazine began to feed off of inventory in its declining years.

THE DESIRE OF THE MOTH. *Satevepost,* 2/26-3/4/1916. †, O, Fiction.

See Book List under same title.

Two excerpts reprinted, *America in the Southwest,* Alburquerque, 1933; a version based upon a scenario by Elliott J. Clawson appeared *Motion Picture Weekly,* 10/3/1917.

Rhodes completed his first try at this story about March 13, 1905.

THE PERFECT DAY. *McClure's,* April, 1916. †, O, Fiction.

THE DESIRE OF THE MOTH. See Book List for, 4/15/1916.

THE RAGGED TWENTY-EIGHTH. *McClure's,* June, 1916. NW, Fiction.

Based upon and a tribute to the Civil War service of his father, Colonel Hinman Rhodes, Twenty-Eighth Illinois Volunteer Infantry.

Reprinted, in full, as an advertising promotion miniature of *McClure's* issue for June, 1916; a medallion of A. Lincoln graced the cover and an editorial blurb on this story said: " . . . a story that goes beneath the surface and tells one the plain, simple facts about American manhood."

THE BELLS OF ST. CLEMENS. *Satevepost,* 6/10-17/1916. Fiction.

Makes most of pp. 191/273, WEST IS WEST.

THE MIRACLE. *Redbook,* July, 1916. NW, Fiction.

Romance in a medieval setting in collaboration with Lawrence Yates. The editorial blurb stressed the better known of the two: "Most of Eugene Manlove Rhodes' writing has dealt with the Southwest. Here he swings to an entirely new vein, and the result is a short story you'll delight to remember."

THE PRODIGAL CALF. *The Silhouette,* Aug., 1916. Fiction.

Signed collaboration with Agnes Morley Cleaveland who gives details in her book, *No Life for a Lady.*

"EUGENE MANLOVE RHODES INTERVIEWS 'THE SILHOUETTE' ". *The Silhouette,* Sept., 1916. *Quien Sabe?*

This literary periodical expired after the two issues listed here. It was published in Oakland, Calif., where Mrs. Cleaveland then made her home which explains Rhodes' appearances.

Various Newspapers, 1917/1923.

It is known that Rhodes' fiction was distributed during this period by Metropolitan Newspaper Syndicate, probably "boiler plate" for country weeklies. Fiction files of this company were not acquired by its successor, United Feature Syndicate, and specific data is lacking. Paul Revier Reynolds was Rhodes' literary agent for some of this period but no information has been available from that source.

THE BIRD IN THE BUSH. *Redbook,* April, 1917. †, W, R, Fiction.

This is my personal favorite of all Rhodes' short stories — *W.H.H.*

OVER, UNDER, AROUND OR THROUGH. *Satevepost,* 4/21-5/19/1917. †, Fiction.

See Book List under COPPER STREAK TRAIL; note time lag between serial and book appearance.

THE BRAVE ADVENTURE. *Redbook,* Oct., 1917. †, NW, Fiction.

Rhodes started this story in 1910 as a memorial to his baby daughter, Barbara, who died that year: ". . . means more to me than all the rest of my stories put together." Based upon the Battle of Shiloh, where his family fought well, this story is hopelessly outdated today and very probably would not have found a publisher then had it not been for the gathering clouds of WW I.

EUGENE MANLOVE RHODES. *Satevepost,* 10/13/1917. Blurb.

Humorous autobiographical paragraphs in the "Who's Who and Why" department of the magazine; graced by a snapshot of Rhodes playing tennis.

WEST IS WEST. See Book List for, Dec., 1917.

THE BATTLE OF MUTTON HILL. *Binghamton* [NY] *Press,* 3/15,16,18/1918. H[excerpt] Essay.

Rhodes' only writing during America's involvement in WW I. An impassioned plea for recognition of the farmer as the front-line of defense. Title based on name of Rhodes' farm in Tioga County, New York, near Apalachin.

NO MEAN CITY. *Satevepost,* 5/17-24/1919. †, R, Fiction.

Based upon an alleged German plot to dynamite Elephant Butte Dam in New Mexico.

GROSSET AND DUNLAP REPRINTS. See Book List for, 3/-17/1920.

STEPSONS OF LIGHT. *Satevepost,* 9/11-10/2/1920. †, Fiction.

See Book List, same title; see Booklets under *Say Now Shibboleth* for "King Charles's Head".
This story was purchased by *Satevepost* on 11/25/1919, almost a year before it appeared.

DR. NICKEL — MR. DIME. *Los Angeles Times,* 5/27/1921. Editorial.

Plea for Angeleños to vote a bond issue for a new library.

STEPSONS OF LIGHT. See Book List for, 6/3/1921.

OUT WEST. *Screenland,* ?, 1921. Essay.

One-page dissertation on the three Wests — in fact, in fiction, in Hollywood.

SAY NOW SHIBBOLETH. See Booklets for, Dec., 1921.

COPPER STREAK TRAIL. See Book List for, 5/5/1922.

THE WEST THAT WAS. *Photodramatist* [later *Story World*], Sept., 1922. R, Essay.

Opening gun in Rhodes' fight against Mencken and His Ilk.

THE TRIUMPH OF THE EGG. *The Stepladder,* Apr., 1923. Essay/Review.

Rhodes on Sherwood Anderson in the house organ of the Bookfellows, Chicago, Ill.; Rhodes was Bookfellow No. 95.

ARE AMERICANS PEOPLE? *Story World,* Apr., 1923. Letter.

Contribution to a symposium stirred up by Rhodes drastic comments in "The West That Was" above.

THE NEW LITERARY MOVEMENT. *Los Angeles Times,* 4/-1/1923. Essay/Review.

Rhodes, at length on Ludwig Lewisohn's *Up Stream* and the school it represented. Thomas Ford, then Literary Editor of the *Times,* was a personal friend of Rhodes.
Long excerpt reprinted in A BAR CROSS MAN.

A SONG OF HARVEST. *Sunset,* June, 1923. H, W, Verse.

AN OVERSIGHT. *The Stepladder,* Oct., 1923. Essay/Review.

Rhodes on "Comrade" Mencken.

UNTITLED. *Dearborn [Mich] Independent,* 12/7/1923. Letter.

Damns Stuart Henry for his review of Emerson Hough's *North of 36;* full discussion of this phase of Rhodes' career is found in A BAR CROSS MAN.

THE MEN WHO MADE THE WEST. *International Book Review,* Jan., 1924. Letter.

Rebuttal of Stuart Henry's review, above, which had appeared in this adjunct of *The Literary Digest;* written as an essay with too many personal references to Mr. Henry, it was toned and watered down by the editors to letter form.

UNTITLED. *The Pioneer,* March, 1924. Letters.

Contributions to a San Antonio, Texas, periodical, praising George W. Saunders for *The Trail Drivers of Texas* and offering comments on the Hough/-Henry controversy.

THE COWBOY IN FICTION. *Story World,* ?, 1924. Essay.

Titled by Rhodes, "The Cowboy, His Cause and Cure;" advice to prospective writers of "westerns" that they devote attention to the cowboy's work and not his gunplay.
Reprinted, *Writer's Markets and Methods,* May, 1933, with omission of this closing paragraph: "You should read George Patullo's 'The Horse Wrangler' about 'little Dick, who never lost a horse,' perhaps the best western short story written, true to life, reflecting all that was best of the cowboy spirit. I don't

know if it has been published in book form. If not, let us make demand that it shall be. It would be shameful that so fine a story should be forgotten."

A DEAR SCHOOL. *Collier's*, 11/29/1924. Editorial.

Rhodes on F. Scott Fitzgerald.
Reprinted, A BAR CROSS MAN.

UNTITLED. *Adventure*, 12/30/1924. Letter.

In "The Camp Fire" section, this extolled the West and its state of mind.

ONCE IN THE SADDLE. *Satevepost*, 4/11-25/1925. †, Fiction.

See Book List under same title.
Note, also, that this ended an almost five year gap in major productivity.

UNTITLED. *Collier's*, 11/7/1925. Letter.

Concerns ownership of the phrase "A fool and his honey are soon parted" which Rhodes had used in "Stepsons of Light" as "A fool and his honey are soon started."

PASÓ POR AQUÍ. *Satevepost*, 2/20-27/1926. †, O, Fiction.

See Book List under ONCE IN THE SADDLE.
As reprinted, O above, the last five lines were omitted by Frank Dearing, thus following the suggestion made by Bernard DeVoto in his introduction to THE HIRED MAN ON HORSEBACK.

RECOGNITION. *Satevepost*, 5/27/1926. H, W, Verse.

Written to and for his wife: "Out of some six bushels, Scriptural measure, this is the nearest I have ever come to real poetry."

THE CIVILIZED MINORITY. *Southwest Review*, Oct., 1926 Essay.

Rhodes' last large-caliber shell at The Young Intellectuals until his *Touring Topics* essays in 1933.

UNTITLED. *Santa Fe [N.M.] New Mexican*, 1927, et seq. Miscellaneous.

From early 1927 until he died, Rhodes wrote many letters to E. Dana Johnson, editor of this newspaper. These letters, or excerpts or revisions of them, were printed by Johnson as he saw fit. No attempt has been made to compile their actual appearances simply because they are too numerous and too unimportant.

THE EARLY DAYS. *New Mexico Highway Journal*, March, 1927. Memoir.

ONCE IN THE SADDLE. See Book List for, 4/29/1927.

HE'LL MAKE A HAND. *Sunset,* June, 1927, $200.00. Article.

Praise of Charles A. Siringo to complement Joseph Henry Jackson's review of *Riata and Spurs* in this same issue. Believed that Harrison Leussler, then Houghton Mifflin's sales representative in the West, engineered this bit of propaganda.

Excerpts quoted by J. Frank Dobie in his Notes to *A Texas Cowboy,* New York, 1950.

THE TIE-FAST MEN. *Cosmopolitan,* July, 1927, $7,500.00 for the four stories therein. †, W, Fiction.

Titled by the magazine "The Bad Man and the Darling of the Gods" which Rhodes considered an emetic.

THE WEST THAT WAS. *Bookman,* Aug., 1927. Essay/Review.

Long appreciation of Alan LeMay's novel, *Painted Ponies.*

IN DEFENSE OF PAT GARRETT. *Sunset,* Sept., 1927, $175.00. R, Essay.

Masterful protest against what Walter Noble Burns did to Pat Garrett's character in *The Saga of Billy the Kid.* Revised by Rhodes for use in his never completed non-fiction book about New Mexico, and this revision reprinted in THE RHODES READER.

A woodcut of Rhodes graced the Table of Contents page of this annual "Old West" number of the magazine with an editorial appreciation of Rhodes by Joseph Henry Jackson, then editor of the dying literary journal and for many years thereafter Literary Editor of the *San Francisco Chronicle.*

NEGLECTING FRACTIONS. See Title, 1928. Essay.

Makes pp. 29/31 in *They Know New Mexico,* A T & SF Ry., Chicago; also contains two paragraphs of humorous autobiographical comments. Limns Rhodes' feeling that southern New Mexico had quite as much to offer the tourist or resident expatriate as did Taos or Santa Fe.

WHEN APACHE KID TOOK A WIFE. *New Mexico Highway Journal,* Jan., 1928. H, Memoir.

An incident from Rhodes' life in the San Andrés Range when he almost made another tally in the Apache Kid's *credits;* contains a letter from Charles Anderson confirming Rhodes' statements about the horses the Kid stole from him on this junket.

Note that this Apache Kid was a Mescalero and not the same Apache Kid who haunted southern Arizona for whom see Jess G. Hayes, *Apache Vengeance,* Albuquerque, 1954.

THE HIRED MAN ON HORSEBACK. *Adventure,* 2/1/1928. H, W, O, Ballad.

Reprinted, *The Turquoise Trail,* Boston, 1928; *The Brand Book,* Denver Westerners, 1945.

This title, like "Pasó por Aquí", has become a generic term in the lexicon of the West.

PORTRAIT OF A PROHIBITIONIST. *Bunker's Monthly*, Dallas, Texas, June, 1928. *Quien Sabe?*

Spasm of anger over contemporary Eastern depictions of the Westerners who voted DRY.

AFORESAID BATES. *Cosmopolitan*, Aug., 1928. †, W, R, Fiction.

Excerpt reprinted, *New Mexico's Own Chronicle*, Dallas, 1937.

TRAIL'S END. *Cosmopolitan*, Feb., 1929. †, W, Fiction.

THE IMMORTALS. *Adventure*, 6/1/1929. H, W, Verse.

This had its inception in an article by Mark Twain, "St. Joan of Arc," *Harper's Monthly*, December, 1904 which may seem incredible.

PEGASUS AT THE PLOW. *Satevepost*, $50.00, 7/20/1929. W, Verse.

Reprinted, *New Voices of the Southwest*, Dallas 1934, apparently without permission.

ENGLE FERRY. *Satevepost*, $100.00, 8/10/1929. †, H, W, Verse.

Reprinted, *New Voices of the Southwest*, as above; *Christian Home*, Council Bluffs, Iowa, 9/26/1929; *New Mexico Magazine*, October, 1929.
The waters behind Elephant Butte Dam now cover Engle Ferry which in Rhodes' youth had been vital to the life of the land where he spent that youth.

THE LITTLE PEOPLE. *Satevepost*, $150.00, 12/14/1929. W, Verse.

NIGHT MESSAGE. *Satevepost*, $25.00, 1/4/1930. W, Verse.

SHOOT THE MOON. *Cosmopolitan*, Aug., 1930. W, Fiction.

MAID MOST DEAR. *Satevepost*, $3,000.00, 8/16/1930. †, O, Fiction.

Purchased, 1948, by Popular Library for anthology use which has not yet materialized.

MY BANKER. *Satevepost*, $45.00, 8/16/1930. H, W, Verse.

Reprinted, *New Mexico Magazine*, June, 1954, in an article by Paul A. F. Walter on the First National Bank of Santa Fe. Evidence in the Bank's records indicate that Rhodes wrote this poem to them, for favors rendered, and then submitted it to the *Post*.

17

UNTITLED. *El Paso* [*Texas*] *Times*, 2/8/1931. Letter.

Appeared in the Book Page conducted by Eugene Cunningham; extolled "Invisible Government" by Samuel Crowther, *Ladies Home Journal*, February, 1931.

Foreword to TRIGGERNOMETRY. March, 1931. Essay.

Triggernometry by Eugene Cunningham; Press of the Pioneers, 1934; Caxton, Caldwell, Idaho, 5th Ed., 1954.

IMPORTANT — EINSTEIN'S UNIVERSE. *Satevepost*, 4/18/-1931. W, Verse.

THE TRUSTY KNAVES. *Satevepost*, $7,500.00, 4/18-5/2/1931. †, O, Fiction.

See Book List, same title.
The story that solved the mystery of Bill Doolin's hideout after he broke jail at Guthrie, Oklahoma.

RELATIVITY FOR LADIES. *Satevepost*, 7/11/1931. H, W, Verse.

UNTITLED. *Hoofs and Horns*, Tucson, Ariz., 8/28/1931. *Quien Sabe?*

Frank M. King, then editor, could not remember what this was nor have the back issues of the magazine for this period survived. That this piece did appear is based upon letters between Rhodes and King mentioning it *en passant*

ADVICE. *Satevepost*, 8/29/1931. W, Verse.

PERSONAL LIBERTY. *Satevepost*, 10/31/1931. W, Verse.

Reprinted, *El Paso Times*, n.d.

NINETEEN THIRTY-ONE. *Satevepost*, 11/7/1931. W, Verse.

THE BALLAD OF EAST AND WEST. *Satevepost*, 12/19/1931. W, Verse.

About bridge hands as featured in newspaper columns; Rhodes had to send a diagrammatic layout of the hands he used in this poem before the *Post* could understand it and, more important, pay for it.

FIRE SONG. *Satevepost*, 1/23/1932. W, Verse.

UNTITLED. *Hoofs and Horns*, 2/12/1932. *Quien Sabe?*

Something about Andy Adams but otherwise unidentified.

THE PROUD SHERIFF. *Satevepost*, 10/1-15/1932. †, Fiction.

See Book List under same title.

MARK TWAIN EMBODIES AMERICAN FRONTIER SPIRIT. *Los Angeles Times*, 12/4/1932. Review.

Uncritical appreciation of Bernard DeVoto's *Mark Twain's America*, Boston, 1932, with a few asides for Van Wyck Brooks. The review carried a photograph of Rhodes!

BEER, ARMED THUGS AND CIVIL WAR. *Touring Topics* [now *Westways*], Dec., 1932. Essay.

A blast at Rupert Hughes, for an article in *Liberty*, and at a concurrent editorial in *Collier's*, suggesting that America abandon Prohibition lest Civil War ensue.

This first appearance contained an Introduction of Rhodes to the readers by Phil Townsend Hanna, editor of this house organ for the Automobile Club of Southern California. Hanna was a most courageous man to publish these blasts by Rhodes which were, for the most part, at complete variance with the philosophies of his Club officers and members.

GEOGRAPHICAL INHUMANITIES. *Touring Topics*, Jan., 1933. Essay.

A chiding, or hiding, of A. Edward Newton, distinguished bibliophile and literateur, for his suggestion in *Atlantic* that the sparsely populated Western states abandon their privilege of two United State Senators apiece.

THE HOI-POLLOI AND THE HOITY-TOITY. *Touring Topics*, Feb., 1933. Essay.

This and the one following were a summation of Rhodesian feeling about the Mencken-Nathan-Sherwood Anderson-Ludwig Lewisohn school and clique.

THE SCORPION ON THE HEARTH. *Touring Topics*, March, 1933. Essay.

THE NEAR BALLADE OF MASTER MINDS. *New Mexico Magazine*, April, 1933. Verse.

A plea that somebody do something that the faceless thousands of the Depression could earn honorably their daily bread. "Even Christy Mathewson couldn't pitch without a ball."

THE GREAT TRADITION — I. *Touring Topics*, April, 1933. Essay.

Comparison between the ideals expounded by contributors to *Civilization in America*, NY, 1922, and the traditions held dear by the men whom Rhodes had known in his youth.

Excerpts reprinted, *They Die But Once*, New York, 1935.

THE GREAT TRADITION — II. *Touring Topics*, May, 1933. Essay.

> In which Rhodes compared the philosophies and practices of the Mellons, Insulls, etc., with those of Huey Long and found the latter's preferable.

BUNK HOLIDAYS. *Touring Topics*, June, 1933. Essay.

> "I would have my country be as kind to a destitute soldier as to a destitute railroad or a destitute bank."

THE TRUSTY KNAVES. See Book List for, 11/1/1933.

UNTITLED. *Saturday Review of Literature*, 1/20/1934. Letter.

> Communication to William Rose Benét's column, "The Phoenix Nest," which included a nonsense verse, "Tuhid Asone."

PEÑALOSA. See Booklets for, 1/27/1934.

DIAMOND RIVER MAN. *San Diego* [*Calif.*] *Union*, 3/18/1934. Review.

> Takes title from that of the book by Eugene Cunningham which was here reviewed.

BEYOND THE DESERT. *Satevepost*, $4,500.00, 5/26-6/9/1934. Fiction.

> See Book List under same title.

FRONTIER FIGHTER. *San Diego Union*, 6/10/1934. Review.

> Rather personalized reaction to the memoirs of an old friend, George Coe, as taken down by Nan Hilary Harrison.

SKY DETERMINES. *San Diego Union*, 6/24/1934. Review.

> The last piece of original writing before Rhodes died on June 27, 1934; his letter to Rev. Ross Calvin, the author, may well be his last writing of any kind.

BEYOND THE DESERT. See Book List for, 9/18/1934.

THE PROUD SHERIFF. See Book List for, 2/12/1935.

THE HIRED MAN ON HORSEBACK. See Book List for, 10/11/-1938.

THE LITTLE WORLD WADDIES. See Book List for, Dec.. 1946.

THE BEST NOVELS AND STORIES OF EUGENE MAN-
LOVE RHODES. See Book List for, 11/1/1949.

GOD'S BADGERED MAN. *Santa Fe New Mexican*, 11/24/1949.
Article.

> Appearing in Sec. 3, pp. 12/13 of a Centennial Edition, this was a completed
> chapter from Rhodes' unfinished non-fiction book about New Mexico that was
> devoted to James S. Calhoun, first Indian Agent in the Territory.

GENE RHODES, COWBOY. See Book List for, Sept., 1954.

A BAR CROSS MAN. See Book List for, July, 1956.

THE RHODES READER. See Book List for, Nov., 1957.

THE LINE OF LEAST RESISTANCE. See Booklets for, Nov.,
1958.

To complete the chronological list of appearances, it is necessary to
give below some titles which, from clippings in various family scrapbooks,
we know were published in newspapers that could not be identified.
"The Golden Gate" — "A Toast" — "Laus Deo! It Is Done" all
c. 1900: "Disillusionment," *c.* 1901, being first appearance of "The
Prairie Farmer" which was reprinted in H and W: "An Oversight" —
"The End of the String" — "More Matches," for which no other data
exists: "The Idyl of Ide" and "A Song for All Poor Sinners," seeking
charity of thought for "Shoeless Joe" Jackson, appeared in Grantland
Rice's syndicated column at unknown dates.

Several unpublished poems have come to light, too. "A Ballade of
Cedar Fires" and "Sally Sings" were written in longhand in a personal
scrapbook kept by Mrs. Stanley Marshal [neé Rhoda Williams] while
"The Santa Fé Trail" which Mrs. Rhodes mentions in her biography
was never published in *Land of Sunshine* for which it was intended.

Only two instances are known where Rhodes completed a manuscript, submitted it and failed to see it in print.

The first of these was "Journeys of a Manuscript" which was submitted to *Pacific Monthly*, June 2, 1911 and returned on December 6,
1911 by Fred Lockley, then presiding over the magazine's lingering
death. It is a supposition that this manuscript, or parts of it, finally saw
print in *Harper's Weekly*, June 13, 1914, as "When the Bills Come
In."

The second instance concerned an essay, "A Committee of One," which was purchased by *Satevepost*, July 2, 1929, for $750.00. This was a violent attack on the current public deification of the bootlegger and the social hallmark of the hip-flask.

Having purchased this tidy package of dynamite, the *Post* evidently took that sober, second look and decided the piece needed a major dose of literary temperance. Rhodes tried but could not make the changes satisfactorily; he then gave *carte blanche* to the *Post* to do the job. George Horace Lorimer, himself, tried his hand at the job to no avail and the piece was killed on February 20, 1930. The payment to Rhodes was not considered as an advance against future work; the *Post* took their error of judgment unto themselves. No copy of this manuscript has been found.

BOOK LIST

GOOD MEN AND TRUE, Henry Holt & Co., New York; August 26, 1910, pictorial cloth; 16mo., 177 pp., Ill. by H. T. Dunn, [Frontis. only] $1.00 net.

The Holt editions, generally, show the year of printing on the title page. The first issue of this edition may be identified by the date [*vii* '*10*] in the pages of advertisements following the text. There was a second printing, *c*.January, 1911, and a third printing in April, 1914. The first page of advertising in this third printing is devoted to Rhodes with his name spelled *Rhoades*.

At Holt's request, Rhodes added considerable padding to the magazine version of this story which has been retained in all subsequent printings. This book version has been adapted for the stage as a three-act play by George Weaver, Pasadena, California, but has not been produced so far as is known.

This title, plates and unbound sheets of the third printing were acquired by the H. K. Fly Company in 1917. There was no printing by Fly but that firm issued an edition using the unbound Holt sheets. About 6,000 copies in all were sold by Holt and Fly.

A second novelette, "Hit the Line Hard," was added to give bulk when Fly contracted it to Grossett & Dunlap which is discussed hereafter.

An English edition by Hodder & Stoughton, February 9, 1923, sold some 22,000 copies.

In inscribing copies of the reprint edition of this book to Eugene Cunningham, famous writer of Western stories, and to his niece, Miss Amy Davison, Rhodes provided background information on the two stories that made the reprint edition.

GOOD MEN AND TRUE

From Cunningham's copy: "John Wesley Pringle, who was half of him my father and half changed to make him a younger man, died in 1908. Leo Ballinger — as Reo Borringer — still lives in Cloudcroft [*N.M.*] and Arizona. George Aughinbaugh is a successful attorney in Kansas City and can be found in directory there. He went into the story without change."

From Miss Davison's copy: "The Judge is real and was recognized very readily in the southwest. We were young together — yes, and friends. Therefore, the name is changed. The shooting match between Broderick and Bransford took place exactly as recorded but in Deming, New Mexico, and for another reason."

Now then! "Judge" or "The Judge" made the accepted references to Albert Bacon Fall throughout his heyday in the Southwest. Thus, it would be a natural assumption to fix Fall as prototype of *The Judge* in this story. This is accented by the fact that Rhodes and Fall were friends in New Mexico and El Paso and remained friends forever afterwards, despite Teapot Dome and everything else that happened to Fall when his luck ran out. However, it seems to this bibliographer that Colonel A. J. Fountain was *The Judge* herein with judicious additions of some of Fall's personal and business traits. The combination would have tickled Rhodes' sense of the ridiculous as Fall and Fountain hardly were friends in life.

In selecting the characteristics for his fictional villain, *The Judge*, Rhodes started the major type-casting he invariably used thereafter for his true villains. They never are men openly and honestly outside the legalities. Rather, they are men of substance, of political and economic power, who bend the Law to their own ends, who profit, yea grow swollen and fat, on the work of men who work with their hands.

In this standard Rhodesian depiction, Rhodes reported what he knew from life — when the men whom he and his family and his friends fought against were the entrenched members of the Republican "Santa Fé Ring" — John Riley, William L. Rynerson, William G. Ritch, *et al* — who controlled the Territory under the overlordship of Thomas Benton Catron. It is necessary today, because of time's passage, to note that Fall fought against the "Santa Fé Ring" and that Rhodes was a trooper in Fall's Irregulars.

Archaeologically speaking, the Turkish Baths where the climax of GOOD MEN AND TRUE occurs were a part of El Paso life for many years, being built between 1900/1901 by Harry Bailey, of Radium Springs, New Mexico as this is written.

HIT THE LINE HARD

From Miss Davison's copy: "The town — truly photographed — is Socorro, New Mexico. Baca and Scanlon are daring portraits. Elfego Baca swore for years that he would kill me for same but relented as the years mellowed him. Neighbor Jones, bearing that name, is long since dead. I have used the lion's head and heart of him — but have given him the great body which should have housed that great heart. In life he was badly used — five feet one, with the shoulders of Hercules and the legs of a dwarf."

It has been a most interesting exercise to compare Rhodes' depiction of Elfego Baca in this story with the portrayal of him but recently inflicted upon an unwitting populace by Walt Disney in his television series about Elfego. *Hoo Boy!*

Another interesting exercise is to compare the "wild Hieland" dialect given MacGregor in GOOD MEN AND TRUE with Stevenson's usages in KIDNAPPED and DAVID BALFOUR. The same exercise may be continued where MacGregor appears in WEST IS WEST, pp. 11/42.

In both these stories, Rhodes employs his favorite device for personal exposition about the West he knew — a young Easterner who gets involved in the plot on the side of the angels.

CONTEMPORARY REVIEWS

Purists may complain about this section which will be found after every book title. Their lamentations quite possibly will rise Heavenward because only the vehicle where the review appeared is shown, not the author thereof. This was done, shall we say, with malice aforethought. Disregarding the inordinate amount of time required to learn the name of the actual reviewer, if such could indeed be learned, it is the intent of this section simply to show HOW Rhodes' works were received into the fold of current literature. These contemporary judgments, rendered then much as they are now under deadline pressures, may be compared with the later appraisals to be found under the section "Major Review and Critical Opinion" for a rough evaluation of how the Man and his Works withstood the changing tastes of the years and how they emerged from the acid bath of perspective that Time brings. Also, this sampling of contemporary opinions may show that the "Western" was not, in Rhodes' early writing career, as literarily suspect as it is today.

Booklist, [ALA] — "While making extravagant demands on the reader's credulity, its breeziness, ingenuity and robust humor will make it acceptable, especially to men."

New York Times — "A breezy and exciting story of the Mexican border is told by Eugene Manlove Rhodes. . . . full of picturesque incidents and dramatic situations. It also has the merit of being humorous."

Springfield [Mass] *Sunday Republican* — " . . . a clever and spirited little story of the Texas frontier and comes very near to being a model of what such a story should be. It is full of action, extremely concentrated and lively and entertaining in style. . . . it deservedly attracted much attention while it was appearing as a serial . . . which possibly accounts, in some degree, for its extreme brevity. It can hardly account for the unusual lightness of touch and gayety of style which makes it ingratiating to the reader. Mr. Rhodes evidently knows the Southwest and puts the wonderful dialect of the residents in its right place as an artificial idiom, namely, which your cowboy can talk when it pleases him, relapsing into ordinary English when he is more serious. The humor is of a brisk and entertaining sort. . . . The tale deserves a wide popularity."

Living Age — "As genuine a comedy of bloodshed as the literature of American manners can furnish."

It is well worth noting here that the *motif* of these contemporary reviews is the humor with which Rhodes clothed his story of violence. Humor was one of the parents of the "Western" when it was born and Rhodes, for an opinion, was one of the ablest users of it; compare his humor with, say, that employed by Alfred Henry Lewis in the WOLF-VILLE yarns. Today, unfortunately, the "Western" smacks overly of ill-digested hunks from Psych. I and only S. Omar Barker, another New Mexican, uses humor in its pristine form when constructing a "Western."

BRANSFORD IN ARCADIA OR THE LITTLE EOHIPPUS,
Henry Holt & Co., New York; Jan 23, 1914, cloth, 12mo., 236
pp., $1.20 net. [Frontis. by H. T. Dunn]

No definite data on number of Holt printings. It is believed that the first issue
may be identified by [*xi '13*] in the pages of advertisements following the text.
GOOD MEN AND TRUE gets a page of advertising facing the verso of the
Frontispiece. This title, plates and unbound sheets were acquired by Fly in 1917. There
was no printing by Fly but that firm issued an edition using the unbound Holt
sheets as RAINBOW RANGE, that title being listed on the d/j of a copy of
WEST IS WEST in Jeff Dyke's possession. This is supported by appearance of the
Fly colophon on the title page of the Grossett & Dunlap edition of this book from
the Holt plates which was titled BRANSFORD OF RAINBOW RANGE.

About 3,000 copies, total, were sold by Holt and Fly in the various printings.
An English edition by Hodder & Stoughton, June 17, 1921, sold some 22,000 copies. The Grossett & Dunlap edition is discussed fully hereafter.

At Holt's request, Rhodes altered the last one-third of his magazine story,
changing the locale of the climax from Owego and Ithaca, New York to New
Mexico where the basic story had been laid. This necessitated changing certain
characters through whom Rhodes was limning his impressions of "Easterners" and
required drastic surgery on the length of this closing section " . . . *for an irretriev-
able loss.*" This revision of the magazine yarn for Holt's publication appears in all
subsequent book appearances. The sixteen closing lines of both magazine and book
versions are identical.

From a note to Retta Badger: "Jeff Bransford's mother was a full-blooded
Sioux; his father a Virginian who came west as an Indian trader. Bransford remembers the Custer Massacre [sic] and how his mother sat by the fire and cried
because the Sioux were fighting the white men and her own relatives were leading
the fight. And he knew Bob Ford who killed Jesse James. Billy the Kid was on
Bransford's list of acquaintances, too. He says 'It was easy to get along with Billy.
All you had to do was give him everything he wanted — barring nothing — and
it was all right. But you could not cross him.' "

The essential accuracy of Jeff Bransford's antecedents may be verified in Lewis
Garrard's *Wah-to-yah* and in David Lavender's classic, *Bent's Fort*. Mrs. Bransford was a niece of Red Cloud, true, but there is doubt that either she or Jeff, her
youngest child, were in the Sioux village that June day in 1876. Bransford was
born about 1867 and was much of an age with Rhodes. He lived out his days in El
Paso as a nightwatchman and similar and was a pretty salty *hombre* until he died.

Bransford made his first named appearance in "A Pink Trip Slip," *Out West*,
January, 1907, although the experiences given him therein actually had happened
to Rhodes on his trip East in 1906 to start his exile from New Mexico. Bransford
was Rhodes' major hero character, or story protagonist, until appearance of this
novel, which, as Bransford was married in it, brought his career in print to a close.

The Prologue chapter, pages 1/26, is based very definitely on the feud between the Rhodeses and the William G. Ritch family over the latter's contesting
and eventual acquisition of the original Rhodes homestead in the San Andrés
Mountains. It was omitted in THE BEST NOVELS ETC. inclusion. Rhodes gave

another version of this feud in a short story, "Check," written with Henry Wallace Phillips.

The creation of Alamogordo by the El Paso & Northeastern Railroad is faithfully recorded in this story where the town is named *Arcadia*.

Certain students of the "western" have taken exception to inclusion in this yarn of Jeff Bransford visiting a ranch and finding a football player's suit which he then wears to the masquerade ball where the plot gets its thickening. Well, Bransford finds the football suit at Baird's Ranch and Gene Baird did play tackle for the State College of Agriculture and Mechanic Arts at Las Cruces when Rhodes was riding that country. Baird, a 220-pounder, was one of the few men who could throw Rhodes in a rough-and-tumble wrestling match and was, himself, a magnificent rider of rough horses.

Speaking as one who knew the single-blanket, single-jackass, singlejack seeker in his native habitat, the pages [143/149] where Bransford transforms himself into a prospector smell vividly of blast smoke and quartz dust.

Serial appearance of this story brought Rhodes hundreds of fan letters and figurines of horses by the score. It was his most popular *Post* story, on this basis, although book sales were, as noted, somewhat disappointing.

CONTEMPORARY REVIEWS

Boston Globe — "The atmosphere of ranch life in the Southwest, as it is known only to those who have actually formed a part of it, has been reproduced with a realism which is truly remarkable."

New York Times — " . . . Jeff Bransford will be an old acquaintance to the readers of Mr. Rhodes' former novel, *Good Men and True*, and they will be glad to meet him again and to find his whimsicalities, his engaging pretense of ingenuousness, and his virile and sophisticated reality almost contantly in the limelight.

"Mr. Rhodes knows range life in the Southwest and he knows the cowboy very thoroughly, even though he does choose, for the sake of better effect, to embroider interesting patterns upon his everyday clothing. But Mr. Rhodes' novels have one quality which distinguishes them from most Southwestern stories, and that is their truthfulness to the various sides of modern Southwestern life. Time was when the range and the roundup . . . summed up pretty nearly the whole of life in that region. And because it was a picturesque life and novels about it found a ready audience, the cattle ranch and the cowboy became a stock, conventionalized theme and novels based upon it were mulitplied until, conditions having changed, they became utterly false to the region they intended to portray. Mr. Rhodes' . . . stories take account of the new face these changes were putting upon the Southwest and they give a faithful picture of many of its phases. His knowledge and his willingness to use it in thus breaking away from time-honored custom in the writing of Southwestern fiction give to his stories freshness, truth and vitality.

"The chapters of his new novel are held together by some slender threads of plot, which the reader will care very little about. He will be much more interested in the personality of Jeff Bransford and that interesting person's exploits . . . and then there is Pringle, who knows some Latin and likes to quote it, who wrote home to his friends from the Denver carnival the story of his journey in three words: Hic — hock — hike.

"Mr. Rhodes' cowboys are . . . much more entertaining, indeed, than they would have been had he drawn them without accentuating their peculiarities or without giving them credit for keener wit and quicker intelligence than can be claimed by most of their tribe. Sometimes he goes a little too far with this injection of individuality into the cowboys character — gets him out of drawing and injuries the illusion. But even then he is entertaining.

"The narrative is charged with the fascination of the Southwest. The author evidently has felt it himself and he has enough of the poet in his pen to make the reader feel the charm of desert and mountain and wonderful sky, just as he has also the capacity to make one feel the sense of fuller and freer life that tingles in the veins of those who breathe the air of the plateau region."

Los Angeles Times — "This snappy story of range life in New Mexico may be termed almost a one-man story, so closely woven about the main character are all of the details. He is not quite a "Virginian," but he is a stalwart, educated man, who has lapsed into the lingo of those about him, and who has the usual habit of men of undeveloped regions of taking some part of the law into his own hands to bring about justice. His lady love is very sweet but rather incidental. The book might be termed healthy and virile, although overdrawn in the possibilities of some of the situations."

Publisher's Weekly [by Fremont Rider] — "The writer confesses himself to be in that unregenerate minority of novel readers who is rather bored than otherwise by cowboy novels. *The Virginian*, for example, no less than its numerous progeny of imitators, left him quite unstirred.

"All the greater praise then to Mr. Rhodes if in his latest story, which magazine readers will know better as "The Little Eohippus," he contrives to entice this reviewer, unobjecting, through to the last cover. He does it because of a real knack of narrative and an evident and genuine knowledge of his subject matter. Nothing in this world, we are sure, is devoid of interest if it can but find a man skilled in its portrayal.

"To be sure, *Bransford in Arcadia* stretches every bond of credulity. . . . But the reader does not pick too closely into the joints of the plot for the very good reason that the author has developed too much interest in his *dramatis personae*. . . . The way he [*Jeff Bransford*] transforms himself in twenty minutes, for the benefit of the posse close at his heels, from a swaggering cowboy outlaw to a blistered, dusty, stoop-shouldered and peaceable miner, is really one of the cleverest things in the book. It's all cleverly written, though."

THE DESIRE OF THE MOTH, Henry Holt & Co., New York; April 15, 1916, dec. cloth; 16mo.; 149 pp., Ill. [Frontis. only] by H. T. Dunn, $1.00 net.

No definite data as to number of Holt printings. In view of the publication date, it is believed that the first issue may be identified by the date, [3 '16], which appears twice in the pages of advertisement following the text. The first page of this is devoted to Rhodes' previously published books.

This title, plates and, presumably, some unbound sheets were acquired by Fly in 1917. There was no printing by Fly although it is believed that the Holt sheets acquired were bound and sold by Fly.

About 2,500 copies sold by Holt and Fly.

A second novelette, "The Come-On," was added when Fly contracted this title to Grosset & Dunlap. An English edition by Hodder & Stoughton, March 29,
1922, sold some 22,000 copies.

It is believed that this story was published in a Braille edition but confirmation
is lacking.

The lead story was built around the political situation in Las Cruces, New
Mexico, during the period 1896/1900, when the cleavage between Democrats, led
by A. B. Fall and Oliver Lee, and Republicans, led by John Riley and Colonel Albert J. Fountain, was bitter and personally violent. To this political animosity was
added the blood-feud engendered by the unsolved disappearance of Colonel Fountain and his son, Henry, in the White Sands.

The story's hero, *Christopher Foy*, is based solidly upon Oliver Milton Lee
while the name *Foy* is taken from two brothers, John and Henry Foy, who prospected and mined in the Organ Mountains during the 1880s. The *José Espalin*
herein is that veritable José Espalin who made a member of Pat Garrett's posse that
jumped Oliver Lee and Jim Gililland at the Wildey Well during the Fountain
trouble and were defeated. Garrett, himself, appears herein in favorable light as
Neuces River. Anastacio Barela, too, is from life and more than life-size here.

In the reprint edition, the second story was added for bulk. A six-man poker
game features the opening section of this story and most of the players can be identified as to their real life counterparts: *Steve Thompson* was Hiram Yoast; *The
Judge* was A. B. Fall; *The Eminent Person* was Pat Garrett; *The Stockman* was
Oliver Lee; *The Merchant* was Ben Levy, of El Paso. *The Transient* remains unidentified. As originally submitted, this yarn contained long biographical sketches of
both A. B. Fall and Pat Garrett. The editors of *Satevepost* deleted these passages
before publication and no version of this original now survives.

Hiram Yoast and his brother, John, had been in and around Tombstone, Arizona during the Earp/Clanton troubles and John Yoast was credited with finding
John Ringo's body and, indeed, suspected for a space of having killed him.

CONTEMPORARY REVIEWS

Wisconsin Library Bulletin — "Another Texas Border story, quite as humorous as the earlier ones and as unexpected in the solution of a perilous situation
which develops with lightning rapidity. Men will enjoy it."

The Independent [Chatauquan] — Under a box heading, *Summer After-
noons:* " . . . has a good, unhackneyed plot. It would make an excellent film
drama of western life, though, in transferring it to the screen, the eccentric and
entertaining conversation of its hero, John Wesley Pringle, would unfortunately
be lost."

New York Times — "The title of Mr. Rhodes' stirring story of the West is
rather too poetic for the general trend of the tale, and is hardly applicable to the
undeclared lover who is far from being a mothlike personality.

"The little story is full of thrilling incident and of humorous talk, flavored
with the racy slang we expect from its locality. The hero . . . is not one of the
pining kind, and his generous manliness looms larger than the pathos of his position. Like its predecessors from the same author, the book abounds in spontaneous
comedy as well as in tense situations and cannot fail of meeting a reception as
hearty as was accorded *Good Men and True*."

WEST IS WEST, The H. K. Fly Company, New York; December, 1917, colored pictorial cloth, 12 mo., 304 pp., Ill. by Harvey Dunn [Frontis. only], $1.40.

This is the only original Rhodes imprint by Fly. There is no data on the number of printings and no one, as yet, has identified the first issue. Some 9,000 copies were sold by Fly.

This, probably, is Rhodes' most unusual book. For one thing, the Fly edition contains, literally, hundreds of typographical errors — omissions, transpositions, misspellings, and punctuation done with a pepper box.

Secondly, the list of magazine appearances shows the number of his short stories that Rhodes wove into the fabric of his disjointed novel. The new material that appears in the Fly edition is to to be found as follows: Pp. 54 - 108 [*see Booklets for pp. 77/92*]:191-197; 220-221: 227-232: 287-304. [Chapter X, pp. 157/171, THE RHODES READER is taken from this new material].

Thirdly, while Rhodes always had trouble with even one love story, he manages to conclude three separate boy-and-girl romances herein.

Library of Congress records indicate that there was a Grosset & Dunlap edition of this book in 1917 in addition to the other edition by G & D which is discussed hereafter.

An English edition by Hodder & Stoughton, May 27, 1921, but no information on number of copies or printings.

Two inscribed copies of this book, both of the G & D reprint edition, shed interesting sidelights on both the story and on Rhodes.

From Miss Rhoda Williams copy: "Please note with what pleasure I dwell on 'they Welshmen' in this book. The Welsh have a high and honorable history. The Roman failed to conquer them, the Saxon, the Dane, the Norman. They bravely sustained a losing fight of 1200 years, this old British stock, beaten but never conquered: they gave their name to Britain: and were pacified only by the accession of the Welsh house of Tudor to the throne of Great Britain. Williams, in Shakespeare's *Henry V*, outtalks and out faces the disguised Henry, and later, strikes Henry's deputy, redeeming hand and glove. It is a good name and a good people."

From Eugene Cunningham's copy: "The geography of this book is highly synthetic — though the details are exact enough. But rearranged, *La Fontana* is Organ Mt. and San Augustin Gap — but lifted up and carried a couple hundred miles N.E. Similarly — Sundown, Sunol, Memphis and Torpedo Mines. But San Clemente is not Organ Camp. It is Kingston, Fairview, Chloride and White Oaks, equal parts, at site of Organ — but the site elsewhere. So, also, in "The Fool's Heart," pp. 181-212, the valley of North Fork of the Percha is mysteriously lifted up and set down beyond the Datils. Similarly, Magdalena appears once as Magdalena and again as Ridgepole — directly across a wide valley from itself. A thing most difficult for any town to do, however gifted.

"Emil James died in 1929. Twice Sheriff of Socorro County and a man beloved. Doc Hughes, poor knave, was killed in Old Mexico at his old trick of robbing camps. Dick Rainboldt [*Will Rainboldt of Roswell*] was killed while still a young man at Roswell. Here — I must stop this.

"Oh, by the way, says one and all, short stories won't sell. But this is all short stories — only I *called* it a novel. And it sold."

An explanation for the studied transposition of places, names and people in the love-element portions of this story may be found in James B. O'Neil's *They Die But Once,* p. 154: "Because, forsooth, in the story are two girls, not exactly major characters, whose descendants might have been saddened or questioned because of certain incidents." Since O'Neil was very close to Rhodes during the last few years of Rhodes' life, and because of his work in promoting the proposed *Bar Cross Edition* of Rhodes' works, this explanation probably came directly from Rhodes.

CONTEMPORARY REVIEWS

New York Times — "The publishers characterize *West Is West* as "the first full-length novel" of its author. Despite a thread of continuity, it might however, be divided into a number of short stories, each complete in itself and each a tale of the miners and cattle lands of Arizona and New Mexico. The stories are filled with what many writers have taught us to regard as the spirit of the West — its excitement, its reckless daring, its readiness to take a gambler's chance; and, withal, its courage, its loyalty and its romance. Mr. Rhodes writes with the abandon suited to his themes. He contrives, too, some ingenious situations, as the double hanging, where each man is innocent of the crime of which he has been convicted, and guilty of that for which his fellow was condemned — all the circumstantial evidence fitting the wrong man to each murder, a significant comment upon such evidence. Those who have enjoyed Mr. Rhodes' former books will eagerly welcome this new volume, and will not be disappointed of their expected thrill."

The preceding four titles, with additions as noted, were issued simultaneously by Grosset & Dunlap at 75c, in uniform size, 12 mo., under the blanket heading ROMANCES OF NAVAHO LAND, Mar. 17, 1920.

There were at least six printings by G&D of these books, the last being May 27, 1925. WEST IS WEST sold some 23,000 copies in this edition; the other titles between 15/18,000 copies each.

GOOD MEN AND TRUE and THE DESIRE OF THE MOTH were printed from the original Holt plates. The novelettes that were added, respectively, to these title stories were set to conform to the Holt type. The result in each case was a 16mo page on a 12mo sheet.

BRANSFORD OF RAINBOW RANGE was printed from the Holt plates with the title changed.

WEST IS WEST was reset by G&D in larger type; the pagination being 386 against 304 in the Fly edition. Whether this was done for the supposed 1917 edition by G&D or was done for this series is unknown. However, G&D retained many of the Fly typographical errors and perpetrated some new ones. They, also, made some minor word changes and made some errors of simple omission in resetting the Fly edition. This, thus, is actually a new edition of this title but no means has been found as yet for determining the first issue.

G&D, so far as can be determined, used the original Holt cover plates for the above titles, except as noted.

CONTEMPORARY REVIEWS

Los Angeles Times — "The romance of the Western cattle ranges has been one of the most prolific sources of inspiration for fiction writers of the past decades. Among the half-dozen writers who have won renown in this field is Eugene Manlove Rhodes. Few writers have caught so much of the excitement, so much of the witchery of the West. Few, indeed, display the keen comprehension of the inner springs of motive that guide the strong men who live and move and have their being of the great wide open spaces of Navajo land.

"Mr. Rhodes, who is now living in Los Angeles, draws upon his imagination neither for the incidents he depicts nor for the characters that move through his stories. These characters are no mere manikins, answering the jerk of a fakir's string, but big, jolly, brawny upstanding men. They are the type of men described by that profane philospher who told his son so to order his life that he could 'look every man in the face and tell him to go to hell.' . . . they are strong men with standards of their own which they are at all times ready to uphold against all comers . . . . in all of Rhodes' work, the love element is secondary and the doings of men, their good deeds and bad, the motives that inspire them and the efforts put forth for the carrying out of their aims, are the solid foundations on which rest his literary and artistic accomplishments."

STEPSONS OF LIGHT; Houghton Mifflin Co., Boston and New York; June 3, 1921, pict. cloth, 12mo, 317 pp., $2.00. [Title page states *with illustrations* which were not included]

The first issue of the Houghton Mifflin books may be identified by the year of first printing appearing on the title page. First printing of this, 5,000 copies; total of five printings, 9,500 copies, to October 2, 1942.

English edition by Hodder & Stoughton, May 26, 1922, at the relatively high price of 7s6d; their editions of the preceding books being retailed at 2/-.

There was no Grosset & Dunlap edition of this book.

It is believed that Fly already had set type on this book when Rhodes changed to Houghton Mifflin for his publishers and that H M Co. bought the completed work from Fly.

Even as Charles M. Russell sometimes concealed a figure from Nature in the background of his paintings, so Rhodes sometimes concealed a minor riddle in his stories. One of these appears on pp. 309 herein, where Charlie See looks curiously at the cylinder of his gun. He had shot two times but *three* bullets had found their mark in Caney's body. The reader is supposed to figure out who fired the third shot; debates on this point have been known to reach unseemly volume.

An extract, pp. 82/86, was reprinted in *Apache Gold and Yaqui Silver* by J. Frank Dobie, Boston, 1939.

Pages 62/72 constitute a definite break in the plot movement while Rhodes delivers himself of an impassioned Jeremiad against current literary "realists" and their so-called "realism." This section explains some of the review comments cited hereafter and, possibly, the lack of any reprint by G&D. It was reprinted as "King Charles's Head" in the booklet, SAY NOW SHIBBOLETH.

No journeyman writer would have permitted his story line to become so disconnected as this essay breaks Rhodes' advancement of his plot. It is doubtful if any other magazine would have accepted this story from Rhodes with this distraction in it. It is doubtful, too, if the *Post* would have let any other writer get away with it. Why the *Post* would let Rhodes do it may be explained in a comment by Mody C. Boatright in the *Southwest Review* [Summer, 1951] during a discussion of Owen Wister:

"George Horace Lorimer, who took over the editorship of the *Saturday Evening Post* in 1898 and frankly made it the voice of American Business, assembled a stable of western writers, including Owen Wister, and through them kept before his readers the cowboy as a symbol of the rugged individualism that had made America great. Henceforth the exploits of the cowboy would recreate the tired businessman and at the same time strengthen him in his steadfastness."

Since the current literary luminaries were as one in disparaging America — the babbitt-warren — Rhodes' blast was not out of keeping with the *Post's* editorial policy.

The description of the Bar Cross horse camp in the opening chapters is a photographically accurate picture of Rhodes' own ranch in the San Andrés which he did, in fact, lease to the Bar Cross as a horse camp for several years. The methodology of the Bar Cross round-up is factually correct, down to the names of the riders with the wagon. *Enriquez*, the story cook, was John Patten, cook at the Mescalero Reservation during Col. Rhodes' tenure as Agent there. In *Pardner of the Wind*, N. Howard "Jack" Thorp relates as fact the same story Rhodes uses here about Patten cooking dinner for forty men in twenty minutes.

Johnny Dines, story hero, was the real life Johnny Dines — *"The most intensely alive and laughing of any man I ever knew."* He was the son of Jacob Dines who settled on the headwaters of the Gila, west of Grafton, about 1881. *Jody Weir*, one of the villains in the piece, used the name of the real Jody Weir, who lived neighbor to Rhodes in Santa Fé in 1927 and still resented his fictional depiction. *George Scarboro* was actually that George Scarborough, noted law-officer and distinguished gunfighter, who killed Old John Selman, the killer of John Wesley Hardin, and was himself killed by Will Carver of the Wild Bunch.

The gold discovery which provided the plot-problem is laid where it occurred in fact — in the Caballo Mountains on the east side of the Rio Grande above Garfield. Encarnacion Silva found dry-washing placers there about 1901 and kept his location secret until November, 1903, when he got drunk in Hillsboro.

Readers of Dee Harkey's autobiography, *Mean as Hell*, will find him in this story, ironically disguised, as both Pete Harkey and his daughter, Edith.

The unresolved romance in this story between Charlie See and Edith Harkey is a romanticized version of the real-life, unrequited adoration Rhodes felt in his youth for Miss May Bailey. Further discussions of this real-life romance, the

dominant influence in Rhodes' fictional heroines, will be found under THE
LITTLE WORLD WADDIES and THE BEST NOVELS, etc.

CONTEMPORARY REVIEWS

Booklist [ALA] — "An episodic western story told with the humor and
philosophy familiar to readers of *Good Men and True*. Appeared in *Saturday
Evening Post.*"

New York Evening Post — "This is a propaganda novel of the National
Security League school. The author has little use for the dissenter, the realist, or
the English language."

[It should be noted that the *Literary Review* of this newspaper then was
conducted by H. S. Canby, Christopher Morley and William Rose Benét who
became the Founding Fathers of the *Saturday Review of Literature*].

Springfield [*Mass*] *Republican* — " . . . departs too frequently from simple
and direct English in the apparent effort to give a literary quality to a story of
simple action."

The Outlook — "A plot story of exciting adventures in the wilds of New
Mexico. Animation in the telling of the incidents of fighting, love-making and
villainy make the book lively and amusing."

Los Angeles Times — "When it comes to description of the great cattle
ranges of the Southwest . . . . has no peer among the writers of western stories
today . . . . men and women are drawn on a vast canvas with that swift, sure touch
that make them seem real flesh and blood creations, sufficiently human to enlist the
reader's sympathy or to arouse his distrust, as the case may be.

"Mr. Rhodes has very definite ideas of the purpose and scope of fiction. So
firmly does he hold his convictions that he devotes the better part of chapter to setting them forth. In this chapter he severely arraigns the work of the present school
of realists, clearly referring to *Main Street, Poor White, The Dark Mother* and
half a score of other books that are loaded down with pessimism in that their authors see life as through a glass darkly and only one side of life at that.

"Mr. Rhodes believes that true realism is to find out where joy resides and
give it a voice beyond singing. . . . "

London Times — "Mr. Rhodes warns us that 'frontiersmen on frontiers never
do anything at all resembling as to motives, method, or result those things which
frontiersmen do in film' and he adds that the 'actual facts are quite simple and
jolly.' His own story of presumably actual frontiersmen is quite jolly, too, not least
when he breaks off in the midst of it to declaim through ten vehemently rhetorical
pages against realism. His heroes do certainly differ from those of the films, and of
most of the printed stories about cowboys. They are more romantic and less sensa-
tional. He can even admit that one of them rides badly enough to be chaffed on the
subject. But that is the limit of the concessions to the actual which Mr. Rhodes can
afford."

COPPER STREAK TRAIL, Houghton Mifflin Company, Boston and New York; May 5, 1922, cloth, 12mo., 318 pp., $1.75.

First printing 5,000 copies; total of six printings for 9,000 copies to February
2, 1943.

English edition at 7s6d by Hodder & Stoughton, March 2, 1923; Grosset &

Dunlap printing from the Houghton Mifflin plates, September, 1924, with some 10,200 copies sold; Hillman Periodicals, No. 46, soft-cover reprint, 1951.

H. T. Webster built one of his famous *Caspar Milquetoast* cartoons around this book in 1944. Caspar is reading the poker-game sequence, [*pp. 273/288*] when his wife says: "There's the doorbell. It's the Mildews to play bridge with us and remember, dear, they never play for anything. I'll put up that leather address book as a prize for high score." Webster's caption ran: "From Eugene Manlove Rhodes' classic poker game to drop the handkerchief."

In this story, Rhodes tried to combine the two halves of his life — New Mexico and New York — without too much success as any reader can prove. However, in his recital of the customs, mores and people of his exile, Rhodes said in print what he could not say adequately to his wife and family in person. The town of *Abingdon* is Apalachin, New York to the very names upon the grave stones.

There are some authorial asides in this story, about natural resource conservation and ownership, which a better lapidary would not have permitted himself. The hero of the yarn, *Pete Johnson*, is the same Pete Johnson who was wagon-boss for the Bar W, out of Carrizozo, when they ran 40,000 head of cows, *mas ó menos*. Both Rhodes and "Jack" Thorp had ridden for him in their youth. *Bobby Carr*, the little boy in the story, suffered some editorial diminution by *Satevepost* in the serial version which Rhodes promptly restored to the book form: "It is from such childhood that the men of my stories were developed."

CONTEMPORARY REVIEWS

The Outlook — "In this story of the cowhand and the mining country Mr. Rhodes, who is a practised and successful teller of Western tales, unites into one romance several incidents of an exciting kind. The action is rapid and one's attention is fully held."

Booklist [ALA] — "A bracing western atmosphere, old ingredients bound together with humor. Men will like it and older boys." [*Starred for Small Library List*]

New York Times — Under the heading, "Summer Fiction Vanguard," eighteen books were reviewed *seriatim*, then a paragraph break and a new lead — "And now for the Western Tales."

"*Copper Streak Trail*, . . . is the best of the few books on this topic which are included in this review. Mr. Rhodes has proved before this that he knows how to handle a Western tale in a restrained and distinguished style, and while his material is essentially light and strung together for purposes of amusement, at the same time he conveys the sense of an intimate knowledge and sympathy with the Western life of his characters that add much to his books. . . . the reader will discover all those things that he desires in a Western novel . . . and a deal of humor. This certainly is the type of book that will go well in the hammock."

Springfield [Mass] *Republican* — "As action-stories Rhodes' yarns stand at the top and by themselves; and his actors are entirely too natural and true to be depreciated by calling them he-men. They aren't he-men, but men."

Boston Transcript — " . . . narrated in such a rambling way, sometimes wittily, but often in such dull fashion that it is difficult to keep the run of the story and to know just what the writer is seeking to say."

London Times — "Mr. Rhodes practises Wild West fiction with a difference. Arizona, as he paints it, is not perhaps more realistic than is usual in such tales, but it is brought into relation for once with another and an utterly different America lying farther to the East. There is a complete change of atmosphere when he transports the reader from the society of miners and cowmen who perform miracles of skill with their revolvers, to that of the comparatively prim inhabitants of a sleepy eastern town. When he endeavours to mix the two and brings Pete Johnson, with all of his cowboy characteristics, from Arizona to Vesper, all illusion of reality vanishes. From the moment of Pete's arrival in Vesper and his confinement in gaol at the instigation of a somewhat Dickensian lawyer, the tale becomes a farce of a lively and entertaining description. It is, as a whole, a curious mixture, the flavour of which supplies a welcome change from that of the conventional Western tale."

ONCE IN THE SADDLE, Houghton Mifflin Company, Boston and New York; April 29, 1927, dec. cloth; pict. end papers; green top; 12mo.; 259 pp., $2.00.

One printing only; 3,500 copies of which some 400 copies were remaindered to Thos. Allen Ltd., Toronto, Canada, below cost. No reprint editions.

The first thousand copies sold were exempt from royalty payment to Rhodes at his own request.

This contained another short novel, "Pasó Por Aquí," pp. 149/259, which at one time was on the supplemental reading list for English Litt. courses at Harvard University.

Miss Rhoda William's [Mrs. Stanley Marshal] copy bears the inscription: "Read second story first. If you never read first story, it will be soon enough."

Inscribing a copy to Charles F. Lummis, Rhodes said much the same thing: "It is earnestly recommended that you do not read the first story. But 'Pasó Por Aquí' is something else again."

Despite his comments above, the title story has much to recommend it in revealing Rhodes' own feelings about the exploitation and oppression of those who worked with their hands. So much so, in fact, that Bernard DeVoto once suggested that Granville Hicks bring out an annotated copy to prove that the Great Tradition had its upholders among the desert individualists.

There is a strong thread of nostalgia for his early days running through the story and the description of the contested homestead involved in the plot is an idealized depiction of what Rhodes had done and had dreamed of doing to his own place in the San Andrés.

Since one conflict in the plot revolves around a mis-location of homestead corners, the following comment by Rhodes seems germane:

"After this story was accepted by the *Saturday Evening Post*, and before it was published, the erstwhile owner of the identical spring I had in mind wrote to me asking help! And did I know precisely where were the cornerstones of the Adell homestead for floods or stock had moved or erased them and the ranch had been jumped by George Henderson on the ground that Adell had mixed up the section numbers and had proved up on a piece of hillside, not on the spring, exactly as in the story. The reason is, of course, that — forty years ago — I had suspected that this mistake had been made by Adell in fixing his location in that whirlpool and turmoil of hills."

When it came to "Pasó Por Aquí," which many critics and *aficionados* believe to be Rhodes' masterpiece, he wrote the following in Eugene Cunningham's copy of the book:

"Tom Powers says, (said, alas!) 'But that fellow never rode that steer.' Tom was wrong. I rode that steer myself — a brindle steer with big horns. And that is exactly how-come I know how to do it. Seven miles, I made on him before he sulled on me. I wasn't particular where I went, you see, or he might have sulled sooner. Where I wanted to go was AWAY."

The flourishing folklore about Rhodes holds that he made this ride just as the story hero, *Ross McEwen*, made it — fleeing from a hold-up. It seems more reasonable to believe that Rhodes made this ride, covering the same course he gave *McEwen* to cover in the story, in making his departure from Socorro after an argument with the Sheriff over the collection of taxes on Rhodes' ranch and livestock. See pages 126/144 in WEST IS WEST for the idealized version of this encounter.

Ross McEwen's prototype was Ross MacMillan — "fascinating rogue — not mean." While *McEwen*/MacMillan never stopped to nurse a stricken family through diphtheria, Rhodes, himself, had been a *volunteer* nurse in a diphtheria pest-house.

Pat Garrett appears herein under his own name in an even more favorable light, by Rhodes' code, than he had played as *Neuces River* in THE DESIRE OF THE MOTH. Coupled with his essay, "In Defense of Pat Garrett," this completes Rhodes' refutation of what he felt was the maligning of Garrett perpetrated by Walter Noble Burns in *The Saga of Billy the Kid*. The change of Rhodes' personal opinion about Garrett, as mirrored in his writings, parallels the real-life change that occurred after the Lee/Fountain trouble when Garrett and Rhodes had been bitter enemies.

Numa Frenger, victim of the story hold-up, was actually Numa Frenger who was Judge of the Fifth Judicial District when this story appeared serially. "He swears he will shoot me on sight. I ask you, is that any way for a Judge to talk?"

There is implicit in this story the regard of a man for his own self-respect concurrent with his proper regard for the self-respect of his fellows that was the essence of the frontier code as Rhodes knew and practised it. Most significant is Rhodes' selection of *Rosalio Marquez*, called "Monte" from his profession which was true to life, to sum up everything Rhodes felt about this code. In Gene Rhodes' New Mexico, it mattered not the color of a man's skin nor the manner in which he earned his livelihood when it came down in life to the nut-cutting stage.

CONTEMPORARY REVIEWS

Saturday Review of Literature — Under "New Books," sub-section, "Travel." "Composed of two novelettes . . . this book treats of a life and characters such as in fiction are usually given the distorted dimensions of the fabulous. The first of the tales . . . presents the familiar situation of the small rancher being hounded for his coveted property by more powerful neighbors. But this beginning soon leads into other channels, which, without break in the unity, contribute steadily to the development of the main theme. The conclusion, though rather too abruptly effected, is the essence of good melodrama.

"In the second story, our own preference of the two, is pictured the gruelling flight across semi-desert country of a bank bandit, who finally takes refuge with a diphtheria stricken family of Mexicans. Though broken in strength, the hunted man remains heroically beside the sick, his better nature uppermost, and cares for them until belated help arrives."

THE TRUSTY KNAVES, Houghton Mifflin Co., Boston and New York; November 1, 1933, cloth; 12mo.; 238pp.; $2.00.

Contains a long [*xviii*] essay written new by Rhodes and not elsewhere published save an excerpt in THE HIRED MAN ON HORSEBACK, pp. 226/231. First printing, 2,500 copies; total of four printings, 5,000 copies, to March 11, 1943.

Grosset & Dunlap edition, same plates, October, 1935, some 6,255 copies sold; English edition by Wright & Brown, Ltd., 1935; Hillman Periodicals, No. 44, soft-cover reprint, 1950.

The first printing of this book was made May 27, 1933, it being scheduled for September release. Due to a mix-up over return of the last proofs by Rhodes, it was not published until the date shown.

The long delay between *Satevepost* appearance, [*4/18-5/2/1931*] and book publication was due, mainly, to an ill-starred attempt by Rhodes to couple this yarn with his later serial, "The Proud Sheriff." He was helped in this effort by Henry Herbert Knibbs.

There is a verve and zest and swing to this story that sets it apart from Rhodes' other long pieces. Many of his short stories and novelettes have this *élan* but this is the only instance where he maintained the pace. Perhaps this stems from the absence of any women, resulting in unimpaired concentration on the masculine characters of the masculine society that had made his youth. It may be due, too, to the fact that he wrote this story back in New Mexico after twenty years of exile and the memory-embers that had kept him warm in New York were fanned to leaping, laughing flames as he relived and recalled those days when he and New Mexico were young — "*There were no gods then and circles had no centers.*"

As B. A. Botkin has pointed out, this story solved the mystery of Bill Doolin's hideout after he broke jail at Guthrie, Oklahoma, for Doolin is in the story, life sized, and Doolin, in fact, make his hideout at Rhodes' ranch in San Andrés.

Submitting the yarn to the *Post's* Tom Costain, Rhodes said:

"Here is Bill Doolin to the life — with some needful exceptions. As five is to four, so is the speech I have given him to the words he was wont to use in the flesh. That was because so much of his slender vocabulary was technical, drawn from the cattle ranges, and hence clouded and obscure to modern readers. Bill Doolin left my ranch six weeks before he was killed and it is much more than probable that when he was killed, he was headed for my father's old ranch to begin life afresh. I was the boy the pony bucked upon — and Bill Doolin shot that horse to keep him from killing me as told in the yarn. I have been mulling this yarn over in my head more than half my life — and, I want to say about Doolin what I said about *Erie* in the story — What a waste!"

Writing to Eugene Cunningham the day after he finished the story, Rhodes reiterated his feelings about Doolin:

"The story is as may be. I think it is rather crowded — and it was one long unending struggle to keep the bloodthirsty from mutual extermination. But be the story as it may, one thing I have right — and that is Bill Doolin. When you read this story — as I want you to — when you come to what *Pres* said of *Erie*, you will know what I feel about Bill Doolin — What a waste!"

To Frank M. King, who had known Doolin, too, Rhodes wrote: "Sure, I know that the $ brand was not allowed. It covered almost any brand. Bill Doolin could not read or write, except his own name! I indicated as much, when he dictated whenever he had to write. And signed by $ instead of scrawling his name. From literary point of view, perhaps I should have said so, in as many words. But the man was my friend and I would not humiliate that friendly ghost."

Erie Patterson in the story is Kim Ki Rogers, for whom Rhodes had worked in his teens, and Kim Ki's manner of attaining affluence while working for the Santa Fe Railroad is reported as the country knew it. The Ladder brand given *Erie* in the story, while not Roger's iron in life, faithfully reports another "maverick" brand that Rhodes had seen grow and flourish in his youth.

When the fictional *B 4* cattle have trouble watering, they but set forth what happened in 1883 when Vicente Villareal, trailing a Y L herd from near San Juan, Texas watered that herd in the railroad pens at Rincon by virtue of his gun.

Preston G. Lewis, "a calm Virginian who looked like Jove," with whom Gene had prospected and worked in his youth, appears under his own name and when he brings a twenty-horse, jerk-line string into town, it is just as Rhodes had done it himself upon occasion. The description of the jerk-line rigging could be embodied without change in any encyclopedia of transportation.

The fictional town of *Target* is, largely, Deming, N. M., and the character of *Herman Lindauer* uses the name of one son to portray the father, Sygmund Lindauer, even unto his Germanic accents in times of stress. Lindauer, a pioneer merchant of Deming, was a friend and more than a friend to Rhodes and in this story he gets his meed of recognition. That Lindauer's Store is still a part of the life of *El Mundo Chico*, that it still is operated by the family, is "Sig" Lindauer's best monument.

Glenn Shirley, prolific Oklahoma chronicler of her outlaws, disagrees over the dates that Doolin was at Rhodes' ranch in New Mexico. Since I am stuck with Rhodes' story and since Shirley and I do not disagree over the essential fact that Doolin was there, the matter seems relatively inconsequential to my purposes here.

CONTEMPORARY REVIEWS

Saturday Review of Literature — Under the caption, "Rough Justice."

"Mr. Rhodes is in his own way a poet. And the story of those trusty knaves who cleaned up Target and ousted the local gang has something of the drawling charm of Owen Wister's *The Virginian*, which, in our opinion, is high praise indeed. A particular passage gave us a thrill such as we usually only get from poetry: [*quotes lines* 1/10, *p.* 114, *H M. Co. edition*]

"Mr. Rhodes is fair to his villain, Erie Patterson proves a brave man at the end. Just occasionally a couple of the characters seem a little too free with literary references; but in general their speech is convincing. Mr. Rhodes writes a story a great deal better than the average Western thriller. He has actually known the prototypes of his characters. A delightful humor distinguishes his story of rough justice."

New York Times — Under heading, "Western Loot."

"A lively and engrossing Western that differs from most in that it is based upon historic facts and, like Rhodes' other stories of the old rough life of New

Mexico, while presented in the form of fiction, is written with painstaking regard for authenticity even in details.

"There are both wit and humor in the telling of this light hearted yet realistic tale, and it rings true. . . . Mr. Rhodes says: ' . . . what I tell you of these unforgotten friends is true telling and no lie. Not the detailed adventures but the arms that mocked at weariness, the feet that trod on fear.' "

BEYOND THE DESERT, Houghton Mifflin Co., Boston and New York; September 18, 1934, cloth, 12mo., 237 pp., $2.00.

First printing 3,500 copies; total of three printings, 5,000 copies, to February 12, 1943. The wrapper of the first printing, at least, carried a brief obituary biography of Rhodes on the back.

Grosset & Dunlap edition, same plates, July, 1936; 10,719 copies sold; English edition by Wright & Brown Ltd., 1935.

It was planned to use W. H. D. Koerner's illustrations from serialization in *Satevepost* but this was not done.

The basic plot-problem herein was taken from the historical difficulty experienced by the El Paso & Northeastern Railroad in finding good boiler water across the gyp flats of the Tularosa Basin. As William A. Keleher has noted in *The Fabulous Frontier:* "The water problem on the El Paso & Northeastern was without parallel in the history of railroad construction and operation in the Southwest." Keleher, like Rhodes before him, got most of his information on the subject from the late William Ashton Hawkins, attorney for the railroad and distinguished citizen of New Mexico. Hawkin's successful plan of bringing water from Eagle and Bonito Creeks, in the Sacramento Mountains, to the right-of-way was the crux of Rhodes' plot mechanism.

In this, his last piece of fiction, Rhodes gave major status to a character who had played minor roles in many previous stories, *Lithpin Tham Clark.* There was much of Rhodes, himself, in *Lithpin Tham* for Rhodes cleft palate bothered him all his life. In his youth, when his own pronunciation of his own name came out either *Dodes* or *Thodes,* depending on the ear of the hearer, it had produced enduring striations on his psyche. So, when *Lithpin Tham* appears in the stories previous to this last one, it is with a certain authorial feeling of "There but for the Grace of God goes Gene Rhodes."

The other contributor from life to *Lithpin Tham* was Clark Hurst, who spoke with a veritable lisp but was much of a man. Hurst, a Lee partisan during the Fountain trouble, was in Hillsboro for the trial of Lee and Jim Gililland. Bob Martin encountered him there and asked, jokingly, "Clark, what are you doing here?" The reply typified the man, "I'm here to make up what the defenth ith thort." Fortunately, Hurst's equalizer was never needed.

In writing what he probably knew, and certainly felt, would be his last story, Rhodes wiped the slate clean for *Lithpin Tham's* past errors, gave him a fresh start, and, incidentally, made him the most entertaining character in the cast.

Rhodes put himself into the story, also, as *Bud Copeland* and studded the yarn with incidents and people from his family's days on the Mescalero Reservation when their bitter enemies were John H. Riley, Johnny Dolan and William L. Rynerson whose control of the country is fictionally told in the acquisition of the *Catorce/Dorayme* country. The killing of *Copeland's* dog in the story actually happened to Rhodes but in the San Andrés and by another man. William Ashton Hawkins, himself, is in the story as *Ellis Fletcher.*

CONTEMPORARY REVIEWS

Wisconsin Library Bulletin — " . . . a writer who knew his western country, never falsified it, and wrote about it with a humor wholly western. This short novel has all of his characteristics, with a good plot and no love interest to interfere."

Boston Transcript — "Seldom does a novel of this type contain so much graphic description, such apparently authentic conversation, such easy, unstudied action that flows rapidly and smoothly as the plot unfolds. Perhaps that is why it is so far above the average so-called Western story."

Booklist [ALA] — Listed, without comment, in January, 1935, issue together with Eugene Cunningham's *Texas Sheriff* and Hoffman Birney's *Forgotten Canyon* for the Western quota.

It is interesting to note that Cunningham's book had 298 pages *vs* Rhodes' 237 pages, both selling at $2.00, both published by H M Co.; also, Birney's book, by a different publisher, had 306 pages for the reader's $2.00.

Readers News — " . . . It contains its share of burned powder, violence and sudden death, but it is tempered with that calmness and exterior casualness which is a true characteristic of the life it protrays. There is no love interest whatever to complicate the otherwise involved procedure of the scheming cowpunchers. . . . "

THE PROUD SHERIFF, Houghton Mifflin Co., Boston and New York; February 12, 1935, cloth, 12mo., 177 pp., $2.00. Introduction [*xxxviii*] by Henry Herbert Knibbs.

First printing 3,000 copies; three printings, total, for 4,000 copies to April 25, 1941.

Grosset & Dunlap edition, same plates, February, 1937, 6,142 copies sold; English edition by Wright & Brown Ltd., 1935; Dellbook 688, soft-cover reprint, May, 1953.

Knibb's Introduction originally was written for the proposed *Bar Cross Edition* of Rhodes' works and was revised and expanded for use here. The story needed more bulk to make a proper-sized book, too. This Introduction contained the first appearance of Rhodes self-composed "Epitaph" which appeared, also, in THE HIRED MAN ON HORSEBACK and THE LITTLE WORLD WADDIES.

Houghton Mifflin turned down the *Satevepost* version of this story, returning it to Rhodes with the admonition to make it longer. However, appearing posthumously, the book version differs only in minor word changes from the serialization.

Technically, this is the weakest piece of plotting Rhodes ever did. There are several logical reasons for this weakness.

As was his custom, Rhodes had taken the actual killing and its cause from life. He could not be too explicit about the role of the woman in the case lest her real identity become obvious: "Hillsboro never knew more than the reader knows — however shrewdly Hillsboro might guess."

In the case of the youngster and his story partner in the Echo Mine, *Old Dad,* Rhodes was reporting one of the many youthful ventures in which he had sided his father: "I was not able to convince myself at any time that *Otey Beach* was in any actual danger. Hence, lack of suspense."

Perhaps because of this plot weakness, Rhodes loaded the yarn with characters and settings he had known. Jack Chandler, foreman of the Double Ess Bar and sheriff of Sierra County about 1900, appears as *"Tip" Chandler*, his nickname from his habit of tippling when occasion offered. Bob Martin sketched him richly in a letter to this bibliographer:

"He was a Texas cowpuncher and a good one. There never was a horse too big or bad for him to climb on — stick the spurs in his shoulders and push forward on the reins. I saw him ride one pitching down a fence line — a 3 foot saddle string stood straight up when he came down and I could see the bottom of the horse's feet and the top of the fence posts at the same time. If he had ever seen this story from the pen of Rhodes using his nickname there would have been trouble."

Aloys Priesser in the story is Aloys Priesser from life — a cultured, educated Bavarian chemist who came to Engle during the mining boom in the 1880s and lived out his life in that country. He was a great friend of Rhodes' father.

Andy Hinkle in this story had appeared previously in STEPSONS OF LIGHT and was, in life, Polk Armstrong of Engle, although using the real Hinkle's name.

Pink Murray in the story is that same Pink Murray who was wagon-boss for the John Cross, J-Half Circle-Cross, in Rhodes' youth. And the story character *Scanderbeg*, used without provenance, was taken from Deputy Sheriff Langston of Lincoln County.

In his settings, Rhodes used the town of Hillsboro, as he had in STEPSONS OF LIGHT, and reported it faithfully and lovingly. The great phantasmagorial house which the killer inhabits in the story is based on A. B. Fall's Rock House out of Three Rivers, N. M., in which Rhodes had lived for many months on his return to New Mexico. Similarly, his description of Apache Canyon and the Caballo Mountains is a virtual blueprint to the region.

A bruise to this bibliographer has been his inability, despite the best efforts of Bob Martin and others, to identify *Spinal Maginnis*, the titular hero, who appears, also, in THE LITTLE WORLD WADDIES group of stories.

CONTEMPORARY REVIEWS

Wisconsin Library Bulletin — "This final novel from the pen of . . . proves to be a fine western tale with realistic background and vivid characterization."

New York Times — "This last tale that he wrote is thoroughly typical of his best work. Probably based on fact (as were all his stories) . . . the tale is told in his own inimitable style — easy, racing, sparkling, humorous and always realistic.

"The deft delineation of The Proud Sheriff . . . adds another noteworthy portrait to this author's extensive gallery of typical fighting men of the old days in New Mexico."

Saturday Review of Literature — Listed in their section, "Over the Counter — The Saturday Review's Guide to Current Attractions," with the comment "First Grade Western."

Booklist [ALA] — Listed five Westerns without comment in the April, 1935, issue. The authors, paginations and common price make an interesting comparison: Max Brand, 301 pp., $2.00; Dane Coolidge, 254 pp., $2.00; Hal G. Evarts, 304 pp., $2.00; Wm. MacL. Raine, 294 pp., $2.00; E. M. Rhodes, 177 pp., $2.00.

Readers News — "Yield yourself in delighted relaxation to the charm of this book. Be with ingenuous people and listen to the humor of their hill-bred words. When you come to what in a sicklier fiction would be tagged "description" do not skip a page; for here the land this author loved comes vividly to life. In swift imagery, simple and heartfelt, he rebuilds America's lost Western soul. The story matter is secondary. The grip on character, land and living backgrounds is unique. Furthermore, in an introduction by Henry Herbert Knibbs, you may learn what manner of man he was who wrote these authentic tales of the Southwest; a man human, humorous, and filled with a faith in his fellows."

THE HIRED MAN ON HORSEBACK, by May D. Rhodes; Houghton Mifflin Company, Boston and New York; October 11, 1938 dec. cloth, 8vo., 264 pp., $3.00; Introduction [xliv] by Bernard DeVoto, "The Novelist of the Cattle Kingdom;" check list by Vincent Starrett.

First printing 2,500 copies; two printings total for 3,000 copies to November 29, 1943. No other edition of any kind although the book was released, apparently, in Canada by Thos. Allen Ltd. Despite the paucity of copies printed, this book is not so scarce as might be imagined.

In addition to the material noted in the preceding magazine list as having appeared herein, excerpts from Rhodes' unfinished manuscript of fact stories about New Mexico were also used.

Evidence indicates that the genesis of this book stemmed from Harrison Leussler's insistence that Mrs. Rhodes collect and publish her husband's letters to *all and sundried*. In the process of compilation and writing, this idea suffered a change of outlook and became a very *gemuechtlicht* biography.

The chronology of Rhodes' life is hopelessly mixed in this book and the information on his pre-marital years is largely hearsay. For a proper understanding of Rhodes' familial and literary life, this book is essential for both what it says and leaves unsaid.

CONTEMPORARY REVIEWS

The contemporary reviews were largely critical appraisals of Rhodes and his work, not of this biography. Thus, these have been included in the section hereafter entitled "Major Reviews and Critical Opinion."

THE LITTLE WORLD WADDIES, William Hutchinson, Chico, Calif.; December, 1946, pict. cloth, large 8vo., map end papers, photo Frontispiece, Illustrated by Harold Bugbee; 234 pp., $5.00. Introduction [xiii-xxi] by J. Frank Dobie and check list, pp. 225-234. Word *wast* for *was* on line 1, page 223. One thousand copies printed and type distributed. Designed and printed by Carl Hertzog.

In addition to material noted in the magazine list as appearing herein, the book contained two poems, "Lyn Dyer's Dream" from STEPSONS OF LIGHT and "The Last L'Envoi" from THE HIRED MAN ON HORSEBACK where they had appeared for the first time. The collection of all Rhodes' verse known at

43

the time in this volume is probably its major contribution to his memory although it seems logical to surmise that the appearance of this volume and its reception sparked the volumes that came after it.

The map used for end papers herein was drawn for Rhodes by Bert C. Broome, *c.* 1929, an ex-cowboy then working for the New Mexico State Highway Department. It was intended for use in the unfinished fact manuscript about New Mexico. A variant of this map, also drawn by Broome, makes end papers in THE BEST NOVELS *etc.*

Dobie's Introduction had an interesting history after first appearance herein. Reset and printed by Carl Hertzog [12 pp., stiff wrappers] " . . . *with a few corrections and emendations*" it was used as a Christmas Remembrance [*1947*] by Frank and Bertha Dobie. As " 'Gene Rhodes: Cowboy Novelist" a shortened version appeared in *Atlantic Monthly*, June, 1949, pp. 75-77. As "A Salute to Gene Rhodes" yet another version, with minor differences in wording and material, made Dobie's introduction to THE BEST NOVELS *etc.* In his *Guide to Life and Literature of the Southwest*, p. 115, rev. ed., Dallas, 1952, Don Pancho says of this Introduction " . . . *plenty of anecdotes and too much enthusiasm.*"

Originally published at $5.00, the current prices quoted by the old-and-rare gentry make a substantial appreciation. The publisher should have stashed away more copies than just the two he saved for his sons.

CONTEMPORARY REVIEWS

Due to the Limited Edition status of this volume, no body of contemporary reviews was amassed other than what appears hereafter in "Major Reviews and Critical Opinion."

The five short stories that bulked this book made their magazine appearances as follows:

"The Bird in the Bush" — *Redbook*, April, 1917; "The Tie-Fast Men" — *Cosmopolitan*, July, 1927; "Aforesaid Bates" — *Cosmopolitan*, August, 1928; "Trail's End" — *Cosmopolitan*, February, 1929; "Shoot the Moon" — *Cosmopolitan*, August, 1930.

As these appeared in book form here, the first above became the last in the book with minor word changes [*made by WHH*] in order to get *Aforesaid Bates*, major character in three of these, *out* of The Little World whereas Rhodes intended this one to be the opening gambit to get *Bates into* The Little World when he began writing the *Cosmo* stories as the first draft of a long novel to be titled THE TIE-FAST MEN. This novel was never finished.

The Little World, *El Mundo Chico*, is that portion of New Mexico enclosed by lines connecting the towns of Deming, Las Cruces and Rincon.

Bates, the central character in three of these stories, started his fictional life as *Aforesaid Smith* in "The Punishment and the Crime," a collaboration with Phillips by Rhodes. He was an invented character although he contained, beyond peradventure, characteristics of men whom Rhodes had known in the flesh.

"The Bird in the Bush," long a favorite of this writer, is the only story that Rhodes classed as "ultra-whimsical." It was included in THE RHODES READER, as was "Aforesaid Bates." This provoked one or two howls from purchasers of the READER which both editor and publisher managed to live through.

In "Aforesaid Bates," Rhodes reported what he himself had done in the San

44

Andrés where his 80-acre homestead gave him control of almost a hundred sections of public domain through some judicious illegalities in the matter of joining rim-rocks together with wire. The drouth conditions which make the plot-problem of this story are taken from life — from the drouth that clutched the *Jornada del Muerto* between 1890/1893. Rhodes' understated narrative of this dry scourge of the Southwestern ranges is the finest recital known to this bibliographer who has lived and ridden through one such cycle in similar country.

The last two stories in this group really do not belong with the others and seem to have been by-products of Rhodes' creative research processes.

In "Trail's End" Rhodes told in fiction what he felt in his heart about several of the breed whom history dubbed outlaws. His fictional bank robbery was blue-printed either from the James/Younger fiasco at Northfield, Minnesota, or from the Daltons ill-starred attempt at Coffeyville, Kansas, probably the latter due to Bill Doolin's familiarity with it and his residence with Rhodes. Where the fleeing robber meets the girl and passes by is a faithful reportage of an incident that happened west of Magdalena, N. M., about 1893, when two fleeing train robbers on played-out horses met two teen-age girls riding home to their ranch: "This is what happened. As they came close one man said to the other: 'Why, they're two girls.' 'Yes,' said the other. They turned out into trails that paralleled the road, as they passed touched their hats gravely and said: 'Good evening girls.' So they went their way. No poor way. Death found them, an hour later, when the posse overtook them. It is more than forty years ago, and in all these years no man has remembered those two dead thieves except with love and pride."

In this same story, Rhodes clearly stated his innate belief as to what was the measure of a man when he has Pickett Boone, the wealthy, conniving, within-the-law exploiter of the Sons of Martha, come to a brutal end through his own avarice at the hands of the one man he had befriended.

In "Shoot the Moon," Rhodes takes his plot directly from the operations in life of a boyhood friend who grew up to organize a gang of thieves with a two-way traffic between New and Old Mexico. In this story he gives prominence to Felipe Lucero, who had been a Bar Cross rider with Rhodes and who was, with his brother, José, Sheriff of Dona Aña County, turn and turn about, for several decades.

Two other interesting facets come to light in these stories. The love story about Charlie See and Edith Harkey which was a part of STEPSONS OF LIGHT was another unfulfilled project on Rhodes' shelf of dreams and the closest he came to realizing it was by putting See into most of these yarns and making a reference, *en passant*, to Edith.

The character of *Joe Gandy*, a fictionally obnoxious deputy-sheriff, is patterned directly on Rhodes' opinion of Ben Williams — one of Pat Garrett's deputies during his persecution of Oliver Lee, loser in a minor gunfight with A. B. Fall, later Chief Special Agent for the A T & SF RR. Yet, in "Shoot the Moon," Rhodes lets *Joe Gandy* die like a man ought to die, like he knew the true metal in Ben William's bowels would have made him do under like circumstances. Because of William's railroad connection, the fictional name of *Joe Gandy* pretty well identified him to anyone in southern New Mexico who had wit enough to recall the term *gandy dancer* and relate it to a Wearer-of-the-Star.

THE BEST NOVELS AND STORIES OF EUGENE MAN-
LOVE RHODES, Houghton Mifflin Company, Boston and New
York; November 1, 1949, cloth, large 8vo., map end papers, red
end; 551 pp., $5.00. Edited with Preface by Frank V. Dearing;
Introduction by J. Frank Dobie.

Bernard DeVoto was scheduled to do the Introduction but, for some reason
unknown here, he did not do it. The inside front flap in many instances shows
where DeVoto's name has been blocked out and overprinted with Dobie's.

First printing was 6,000 copies. Apparently some copies of publisher's uncor-
rected proofs were bound in limp wrappers, per item 613, catalog 24, E. W. Laten-
dorf, Mannado's Bookshop, New York. This book was OP for many years but can
be acquired now, evidently in a second printing for which this bibliographer has
no data whatsoever, at $5.50 per copy.

SUNSET LAND, Dell Publications soft-cover reprint, July, 1955, contains
Dobie's Introduction plus GOOD MEN AND TRUE, BRANSFORD IN AR-
CADIA and THE TRUSTY KNAVES. The remainder of the contents in this volume, with exception of the narrative essay "Peñalosa," were scheduled for reprinting by Dell in 1956. This has not been done, so far as is known, which may be due
to the departure of Don Ward from the Dell organization.

The major inclusions in this collection have been discussed previously as they
appeared in book form. Certain aspects of the four short stories herein seem to war-
rant presentation.

"Consider the Lizard" always has been a favorite of this Rhodesian and its
popular excellence is best indicated by its inclusion in the recent [1954] The Saturday Evening Post Treasury. The factual basis of this yarn is very true to life,
stemming from John Greer's single-handed hold-up of an El Paso & Northeastern
passenger train between Tularosa and Alamogordo. Tom Hall, a friend of Rhodes
and fellow-partisan of Oliver Lee, was killed in a fight with John Greer, his
brother, Ted, and one John Gates at the old Jacob Dines ranch, then a part of the
V Cross T, in 1914.

In "The Perfect Day," Rhodes had a good time for himself depicting the dis-
comfiture of a group of city-slicker con men by a cowpuncher who had a lot of
Gene Rhodes in his fictional makeup. This subjective approach conceals a basic
Rhodesian theme — the conflict between the exploited West and the exploiting
East — which came out most clearly in COPPER STREAK TRAIL and ONCE
IN THE SADDLE.

"Beyond the Desert," which makes pages 11/42 in WEST IS WEST, has
been discussed bibliographically in the magazine list. It is worth noting, however,
that the Prologue which was added to the McClure's version for WEST IS WEST,
has been omitted here and, in fact, is not used in any of the reprint appearances
listed.

Most interesting is the comment made by Jack Schaefer, the Shane-fame
writer, when he included this story in his recent [1955] anthology OUT WEST:
"Canvass the really ardent readers of westerns and about every one in three will
turn out to be a passionate Rhodesian. The man's writing stimulates fanatacism,
cultism. To the faithful, he could do no wrong. They cherish every word he wrote.
They are ready to jump out fighting at the suggestion his short novel, Pasó Por

Aqui, is not the finest western story ever written. Certainly he mastered his material as few others in the field, in any field, have done. The substance of his stories is authentic, as it should be since he lived much of it himself, and over this he cast a glow of creatitve imagination. The Rhodes country is lower Arizona and New Mexico. But it is not the real Arizona and New Mexico. It is the Rhodes country, a never-never land that begins with reality and is transformed and highlighted and made completely his own somewhat as Faulkner has done with that unpronounceable county in Mississippi. His individual books are hard to find — the cutlists have grabbed all readily available — except some that have been reprinted in paperback editions, but a good starting collection appeared in 1949 with the title: *The Best Novels and* . . . Probably no two Rhodesians would agree that those included are precisely "the best" — except, of course, for *Pasó Por Aqui.* But all his stories are superb reading. This one gives you MacGregor, Sandy Macgor of Black Mountain, the sun-god hero with a difference, a man you will not easily forget."

It is impossible not to rise to the Rhodes/Faulkner bait dangled by Mr. Schaefer simply because this bibliographer lays claim to be the only writer of Western-pulp who ever had William Faulkner for a Scoutmaster. What Schaefer says about the transmogrification practised by both Rhodes and Faulkner is true and yet, even as Bob Martin or "Dallas" McCombs, even myself, can identify Rhodesian characters in life, so could my father name the characters in the early Faulkner pieces that appeared before he rode down that trail where all pony tracks point just one way. What both took from life they disguised but thinly and Rhodes' transparencies are more obvious because his prose is not convoluted, because he, himself, was a much less complex organism than Faulkner though no less true to the stock and times that produced him.

The title of "Maid Most Dear" comes from the poem by Jean Ingelow: *"Oh, maid most dear/I am not here/I have no place apart//No dwelling more on sea or shore/ But only in thy heart."* It was in Rhodes' mind as early as 1920 as the title for concluding the love story in STEPSONS between Charlie See and Edith Harkey. When he finally used it here, the love story between Eddy Early and Eva Scales again was patterned after his own early romance in Mesilla/Las Cruces with May Bailey, although the heroine's name was taken from life — a girl he saw but once, near Grafton, N. M., when she was seven and he was seventeen.

His story villains, the K P gang, are based upon the Wild Bunch when they were working for Captain William French on his W S outfit near Alma, where the story is laid, although Rhodes changed their style and mannerisms to make them city-gangster types. *Tom Copeland,* in the story, is patterned on either Butch Cassidy or Black Jack Ketchum — *no le hace* for Rhodes admired both men. Too, when in the story he has *Bud Wilson* say that *Fritz Aude* settled Shard Springs, why it was Fritz Aude himself who did settle Shard Springs and still lives at this writing.

Rhodes had a great personal affection for this story as " . . . *showing more clearly than any other of mine what is implicit in all my stories — the elder ethics, the hope and honor we strove for in that vanished past."* Writing to another admirer who expressed her doubt that many readers would know the significance of "Maid Most Dear," Rhodes replied: *"It is worse than that. Not many today know what maid means."*

The one poem in this collection, "The Hired Man on Horseback," was, basically, a ballad of comparison between the men he had known and the men who infested the writings of the current poo-bahs — Lewisohn, Anderson, Drieser, Waldo Frank, *et al* — who labelled themselves *The Civilized Minority*, *The Revolting School*, *The Young Intellectuals*. Publication of the poem was delayed for many months while the editor of *Adventure* tried unsuccessfully to have Rhodes delete, or change, the five lines beginning "The Proud Young Intellectuals . . . " and ending with "They smile at faith and honor . . . "

In the latest edition of his *Guide to Life and Literature of the Southwest*, Don Pancho Dobie dubs this " . . . a long poem of passionate fidelity to his own decent kind of men, with power to ennoble the reader, and with the form necessary to all beautiful composition. This is the sole and solitary piece of poetry to be found in all the myriads of rhymes classed as 'cowboy poetry.' "

CONTEMPORARY REVIEWS

Library Journal — "A banquet of regional writing is served in this collection, but like the speeches at most banquets it is too much of the same thing. . . . The rugged U.S. Southwest is Rhodes' oyster, and his cowboys and dude characters are generally convincing. His descriptions provide realistic but sympathetic background for the always active experiences of the mildly heroic men of the Southwest. Readers seeking western fiction will not be so satisfied as readers seeking Southwest regional atmosphere."

The Nation — Under the heading, "Books in Brief:"

"Their contrived plots and conventional sentiment make these Westerns, mostly written for the *Saturday Evening Post*, seem pretty dated, but they give the genuine local color of Alamogordo County, [*sic*] New Mexico, . . . The cowboys are not wholly stereotypes and Rhodes is a master hand at a chase or a hide-out. The best one, 'Pasó Por Aquí,' would make a refreshing change from Bret Harte as an anthology piece."

New York Herald-Tribune — Under section, "Reprints, new Editions:"

" . . . As many, but not yet enough, readers know, Rhodes wrote the best of all fiction concerned with cowboys. He had been a cowboy himself, knew and loved the cowboy world, and insisted on writing it at first hand, not as countless writers wrote out of the slipshod tradition of 'westerns,' full of stereotypes in character, situation and language. . . . his work, which pleases cowboys who know it is truthful, no less pleases good judges of fiction who realize that Rhodes' stories must be true or they could not be so convincing and satisfying."

GENE RHODES, COWBOY by Beth F. [*Mrs. Donald*] Day Julian Messner, Inc., New York; in Canada by The Copp Clark Co. Ltd.; Sept., 1954, dec. cloth, 12 mo., patterned end papers, 192 pp., $3.00. Ill. by Lorence F. Bjorklund.

Intended for the 8-12 age group, this book fulfils its purpose. Mrs. Day has woven a vivid story line about Rhodes' boyhood and early years in New Mexico which she based on material contained in his early stories and novels and several interviews with Mrs. Rhodes. " . . . I worked out a fictionalized story — one which I hope is true to the man. My object, as Frank Dobie once said about a book of his, was not so much to record exactly what happened, as what might have happened."

The liberties which were taken with persons, places, dates and happenings, do not violate the boundaries Mrs. Day established for herself.

CONTEMPORARY REVIEWS

None seen nor sought.

A BAR CROSS MAN by W. H. Hutchinson. University of Oklahoma Press, Norman, Okla.; July 23, 1956, cloth, 8vo., index, illustrations, check-list; 400 pp., $5.00.

First printing, 3,312 copies; no others to time of this writing, December 5, 1958.

Not even this bibliographer is foolhardy enough to comment critically upon this book, which was made possible by an initial grant-in-aid from Rockefeller Funds administered by the Henry E. Huntington Library. Work began on the research in October, 1952 and the first draft of the manuscript was delivered to the publisher in July, 1954. This was then rewritten and revised before acceptance which, as it seems to this writer, was due largely to the insistence of Walter Prescott Webb who acted as *Reader* for the publisher.

It was the author's intent to provide a comprehensive and readable study of the environment that moulded 'Gene Rhodes and then sustained him all of his life. Having provided this background, including necessary factual material for the time-intervals into which Rhodes' life fell, it was the intent then to let Rhodes speak for himself through selected correspondence and relatively unknown essays.

This book made Rhodes the *only* writer of "Westerns" to be the subject of not one but two biographies. Considering the part he played in making the "western" acceptable, considering the role, albeit a minor one, he played in American literary life for a quarter-century, this fact does not seem incongruous.

CONTEMPORARY REVIEWS

Frankly, beyond reading the clippings sent by the publisher's Sales department, no great attention has been paid to the opinions expressed about this book. It was an honest job on the part of both author and publisher and that is all that seems important.

THE RHODES READER, edited with an Introduction by W. H. Hutchinson. University of Oklahoma Press, Norman, Oklahoma; November 15, 1957, cloth, 8vo., illustrated map end papers; 316 pp., $5.00.

First printing, 3,412 copies; no other printing to time of this writing, December 5, 1958.

Contains fifteen fiction pieces and essays, many of which never had been printed in book form; also contains a revision of Hutchinson's essay, "Virgins, Villains and Varmints," which J. Frank Dobie was kind enough to dub " . . . certainly, the finest thing written on the Western story as a type of literature." That remark is wages enough.

Should there be another printing or edition, the *first* may always be identified by the fact that the dedication is to F. Bourn*e* Hayne rather than to F. Bourn Hayne which is correct and was correctly set on the page proofs returned to the editor. How this mishap occurred between proofs and print flummoxed all concerned.

In selecting the pieces that make this book, it was the editor's intent to get the keystones of Rhodes' abiding love of his country and his people between covers. Some of the inclusions may seem technically inferior to other pieces by Rhodes but, to be as cold-blooded as it is possible to be, it seems to this writer, over a year later, that the book stands up as fulfilling the original intent.

CONTEMPORARY REVIEWS

A file folder stuffed with clippings attests that the book was reviewed, possibly even read, by a great many people. Nothing yet seen adds or detracts to Rhodes' stature which explains the lack of any excerpts here.

SPECIAL EDITIONS

The Council of Books in Wartime published 1324 titles in a special format for distribution to the Armed Services. The largest identifiable bloc of titles, 160 in number, were "westerns." Five of Rhodes' novels were represented in this group:

G-190 — *The Trusty Knaves*, 40,000 copies
H-212 — *Beyond the Desert*, 81,893 copies
J-271 — *The Proud Sheriff*, 95,168 copies
K- 8 — *Stepsons of Light*, 95,000 copies
M- 6 — *Copper Streak Trail*, 108,218 copies

These all were Houghton Mifflin titles for which the plates were available. The plates of the Holt/Fly books, although acquired by Rhodes in 1928, could not be located for this series and, in fact, have disappeared completely from family or publisher's knowledge.

BOOKLETS LIST

SAY NOW SHIBBOLETH, The Bookfellows, Chicago, Ill.; December, 1921, ½ linen, small 12mo., 55 pp., $1.25.

This was printed by The Torch Press, Cedar Rapids, Iowa; verso of titlepage bears legend: "Of this first edition 400 copies have been printed in the month of December, 1921." It is not believed that there were additional printings. The booklet sold very slowly, being advertised in *The Stepladder*, monthly organ of The Bookfellows, from June, 1922 to August, 1926, both as a single item and as a part of combination offers.

It contained three essays: "Say Now Shibboleth" from *Satevepost*, April 22, 1911; "King Charles's Head" from pp 62-72 of STEPSONS OF LIGHT; and "The Gentle Plagiarist" from *Harper's Weekly*, June 6, 1914, where it was titled "When the Bills Come In."

The Stepladder, September, 1922, said this: "This is a volume of *The Little Bookfellow* series, and contains three essays by one of America's master humurists. The title essay is so good that since the publication of this volume it has gone into a highschool text-book made up of essays of permanent value. Vincent Starret says: 'By rights, this book should be your best seller.' Packed full of humor, every page glittering, there is no question but it would make an acceptable and valued gift for any person old enough to read and laugh."

The high school text referred to above was *Present Day Essays*, Edwin Van B. Knickerbocker, editor; Holt, NY, 1923. In his critical discussion of the essay, pp. 345-346, Knickerbocker had this to say: "To the style is due much of the charm of this delightful essay. The style perfectly fits the attitude and spirit that the essayist assumes. It is often colloquial, and affords an excellent illustration of the difference between a colloquial manner adapted to suit an attitude, and a colloquial manner that is a writer's only mode of expression. The one is art, the other a conscious pose or worse."

PEÑALOSA, Writer's Editions, [*The Rydal Press*] Santa Fé, New Mexico; Jan. 27, 1934, dec. wrappers, 20.9 cm., 34 pp., $1.00. With a Foreword by Alice Corbin Henderson, this edition was limited to 500 copies, all autographed by Rhodes.

This was a separate printing of the "Barnaby Bright" chapter, pp. 77-92, from WEST IS WEST, where it first saw print.

Reprinted in THE BEST NOVELS, etc., without Mrs. Henderson's foreword.

The best comment on PEÑALOSA is found in two letters from Rhodes to Alice Corbin Henderson, who had conceived the idea of publishing it, underwrote the cost and contributed the Foreword. The excerpts are combined here for readability.

"It is a delightful surprise to me that you contemplate having the "Peñalosa" chapter brought out as a brochure. It is one of my dearest wishes and has long been that. WEST IS WEST started from that. The first sentence written of that book was 'Then the sad mists rose, and night, and blotted out that sail.' It was my hope to suggest to the reader the 'continuity of the generations' as C. E. Scoggins puts it in the last sentence of *Tycoon.*

"It should be said that Fuentes is pure invention — and all scenes where he appears. The rest as to Peñalosa is pure history — at least, is taken verbatim from the account of Nicolas de Freitas.

"Peñalosa is condemned of historians. All they know of him is what the Inquisition says — that tried him. Curiously enough, Malignant Protestants who are most bitter against the Inquisition take the Inquisition at face value. The Inquisition which took his wealth away from him, admittedly and by their own record, for opposing their own harsh methods of conversion — that is to say, cruel force in New Mexico — and for 'leaps of the tongue against the Lords Inquisitors and some absurdities that bordered upon blasphemy.' I have obligingly supplied the words of these blasphemies in Peñalosa's supposed speech about sun-worship. The explanation is easy. The Inquisition had to save its face. Their attack upon Peñalosa was confined to one thing — his disputed march to the Northeast. The Inquisition declared that Peñalosa did not make this march. They gave as their reason — *that his account of the country tallied with Coronado's account!*

"Peñalosa may have lied. And the Inquisition may have had private advices of which we know nothing. But the above is all that appears in *the record.* The lamb has muddied the stream from which the wolf drank.

"I am not quite such an ass as to believe that a charge is a lie because it was made by the Inquisition. But I am confronted with the choice whether I am to give the benefit of the doubt to Peñalosa or to the Inquisition. I give it to Peñalosa — mainly, I confess — because it suits my style of beauty. But also because one thing is certain: this was the first man in America — if not in Christendom — with spunk enough to oppose the Inquisition. So I shall admire him, even if it be proved that he was a Dr. Cooke.

"As for Bancroft's history factory — that is easy too. They were tired historians. The only documents pertaining to the case were the records of Peñalosa's trial. They accepted them at face value, gladly, and went to bed with the virtuous feeling of something accomplished — something down. Other historians followed Bancroft. Voila! Also, historians consider 'documented' a synonym for 'proven.' As if a man could not lie as well on paper as by word of mouth. I do mine better on paper, myself."

Don Diego Dionisio de Peñalosa Briceño was governor and captain-general of New Mexico, 1661/1665. Interested readers may compare Rhodes' facts with the account of Peñalosa given by Bernard DeVoto in his *Course of Empire.*

THE LINE OF LEAST RESISTANCE, published with personal comments by W. H. Hutchinson, Chico, Calif.; December 22, 1958, dec. wrappers, 8vo., 78 pp., $4.00.

Limited edition of 500 numbered copies signed by the publisher; designed and produced by Hurst & Yount, honest printers of Chico, Calif.

The two cover drawings by James Bodrero seem outstanding to this writer. Collectors may recall Bodrero from the woodcuts he did for Hibberd's reprint of Horace Bell's *Reminiscences of a Ranger.*

This is the *Satevepost* serial of the same title. With its publication the task of restoring Rhodes' to print that began in 1946 with THE LITTLE WORLD WADDIES has been completed for all practical, let alone reasonable, intents and purposes.

BOOK AND BOOKLET NOTES

These comments may inspire howls of outrage or peals of bubbling mirth from collectors and dealers who have their own opinions and cherish them to keep them warm.

The first issue of the three books by Holt may be classed as RARE. So may THE LITTLE WORLD WADDIES, SAY NOW SHIBBOLETH and PEÑALOSA.

What to say about the Fly printings of WEST IS WEST requires a wider knowledge and more sensitive antennae than can be claimed here.

The first issues of the Houghton Mifflin books range from *Scarce* to *Very Scarce* depending upon capillary attraction in the cataloguer.

The G & D reprints, even the early books, seem fairly common although *Scarce* in good condition.

Legible, non-fragmented dust jackets of any book and issue are *Rare.*

No comment can be made on the English reprints.

THE HENRY WALLACE PHILLIPS' BOOKS

By his own statement, Rhodes had a hand in four books by Phillips without name or other credit.

In one of these, *Trolley Folly*, the evidence is irrefutable since it contains two of the signed Rhodes/Phillips collaborations from *Satevepost*. Additionally, it contains another short story, "The Little Canoe," in which Rhodes seems implicated on the internal evidence.

The evidence seems irrefutable, also, in *Red Saunders' Pets and Other Critters*, for the short story, "A Touch of Nature."

In *The Mascot of Sweetbriar Gulch*, [Bobbs-Merrill, 1908.] the evidence is internal. That Rhodes had a hand up to his elbow in this book is a statement made after long and painful study of both men concerned. Phillips, alone, never stepped out of the geographic locale he knew first-hand, the Northern Plains/Missouri River headwaters, any more than Rhodes abandoned the country he knew first-hand for his own settings.

When you find Phillips using Southwestern settings, Border Spanish and technical details of hard-rock mining, [Phillips was a placer man, himself] plus displaying an impassioned affection for steam locomotives, the evidence becomes slightly circumstantial, like finding a drowned cat in a cream jug. When these are intertwined with Bowery argot, Sioux vocabulary and flora of the Northern Plains, plus the refined sense of situation comedy that was Phillips' trademark, the conclusion of collaboration becomes inescapable. There is one more point. Phillips, if anything, was more awkward at handling women in his stories than was Rhodes. When you find Rhodes' frontier-Gothic romanticism in a Phillips' story, it strikes a familiar note. This is the summarized evidence upon which Rhodes' implication in *The Mascot of Sweetbriar Gulch* is based.

As to the fourth book, the most likely candidate is *Mr. Scraggs*. [McClure, Phillips and Co., 1906]. Here the feeling of conviction is on the wane. The styles of the two men are so miscible, particularly in Rhodes' early stage, that this book, has a homogeneity lacking in *The Mascot*.

Phillips' other two books, *Plain Mary Smith*, 1905, and *Red Saunders*, 1902, are such that it would take a foolhardy form of partisanship to make any Rhodesian claims.

Phillips' literary career was comparatively brief, 1899/1914, but his effect upon Rhodes cannot be overestimated. "Henry Wallace Phillips — may his soul rest in peace — and I wrote some stories together. He was a master and I was his pupil. In all these cases the original story was mine, the polish and finesse were supplied by Phillips. He was a wonderful man and writer."

A personal opinion holds *Red Saunder's Pets and Other Critters* to be one of the most outrageously and uproariously funny collections ever between boards. Phillips richly deserves recognition for his place in the ranks of those writers who pioneered the so-called "western story" as a story of humor. To compound the felony of opinion, he far surpasses O. Henry, Bret Harte or Alfred Henry Lewis in this their chosen field.

In an interview with Rupert Hughes, [January, 1953] he stated that Phillips was a commercial artist in New York City, known as "Monkey" Phillips for his animal specialities, before he turned to writing at Hughes' suggestion and with Hughes' assistance. Their first collaboration, according to Hughes, was the short story "Across the Great Divide" of which Rhodes speaks highly in his essay, "The West That Was." Hughes said, also, that Phillips was the wittiest man he ever knew with a note-taking eye.

THE UNFINISHED MANUSCRIPT

Barring his essays and his verse, Rhodes' non-fiction is remarkable by its absence. This may be explainable by his statement that he was "Telling as fiction what I could not repeat as fact." His one great venture into the non-fiction field was his projected Old Timers in New Mexico — "the half-history of half a state."

Rhodes embarked on this venture largely through the blandishments and applied pressures of Harrison Leussler, western sales representative for Houghton Mifflin and E. Dana Johnson, editor of the *Santa Fé New Mexican*. The time he invested in this venture and its eventual outcome are best expressed in two letters to Ferris Greenslet, editor-in-chief of Houghton Mifflin.

Alamorgordo, New Mexico, March 12, 1928
"Dear Greenslet:

"It is to announce that the remorseless and implacable Leussler is to have his way — and I am committed to that book with the assistance of Clem [ent] Hightower. With great difficulty I refrain from inflicting details upon you. But I want to stipulate. There *must* be maps, which I can furnish.

"Mr. Leussler was kind enough to say that there was no other instance where a participant — or did he say an accessory? — had the skill in handling words to tell the tory properly. In fact, that is not half of it. The old timers will talk to me. They will tell me — as another old timer, with their own ethics — what they would not tell to any other writer — and all because I am one of themselves. As for instance — the killing of Apache Kid by Charley Anderson, Walter Hearn, Bert Slinkard and others. Writing people have been trying to get this story for years and didn't get a word. The boys volunteered to tell it to me.

"It will be an enormous task to hunt up the old timers to vertify—all the way from Jim East in Tucson, Arizona, to Charlie Goodnight at Goodnight, Texas. The boys! Goodnight is 88. Jim East is 80. Cole Railston is 67. Johnny Dines and myself [59] are the youngest of the bunch.

"Mr. Leussler seems to think this book would sell well. Decently, *perhaps*. Not more. Such a book, stuffed with lies and hokum, lipsticked, and rouged and belladonnaed, might sell. But the natural complexion — I think not. And lying is out of the question. The boys would catch me. — Yours tediously,"

The second letter was written by Mrs. Rhodes in early July, 1934, from Pacific Beach, California, their last residence:

"Dear Mr. Greenslet:

"I thank you for your sympathy. Mr. Knibbs and Mrs. Fiske have been so kind, but for that I don't think I could ever have carried on. [Mrs. Rhodes just had returned from taking her husband's body to New Mexico for burial. Henry Herbert Knibbs, himself a writer of magnificent "westerns," was a devoted friend of Rhodes. Mrs. Turbese Lummis Fiske was the daughter of C. F. Lummis, who had given Rhodes his writing start and his first valid instruction in the art.]

"I am so deeply sorry to tell you that while the Old Timer book was all but completed, he had even got a title he liked better, *The Silent Past*, he was still carrying the thing in his head, as his ruinous custom was, and only the little scrap you have in your office was all that was typed. When he sat down to write a story, it was practically written. I think this was why writing was so intensely hard for him, but he didn't seem to be able to do it any other way. I am heart broken for he was the only man with all this inside information. We had travelled hundreds of miles to verify it, so it would be first hand instead of hearsay.

Thanking you again for your nice letter, I am Yours sincerely, May D. Rhodes."

The surviving remnants of this venture are now in the Rhodes Collection, Henry E. Huntington Library. Among them is the Table of Contents covering the thirty-two chapters Rhodes had in mind. From the chapter titles, it has been possible to reconstruct at least something of what Rhodes had in mind; chiefly, he was concerned with the settlement of the *Jornada del Muerto* and what he regarded as its tributary parishes, the Black Range/Mogollon complex and the Tularosa Basin. There were to have been chapters on certain aspects of the Lincoln County War, including Buckshot Robert's fight at Blazer's Mill; a chapter on Elfego Baca's fight at Middle Plaza; a revised and expanded version of his previously published "In Defense of Pat Garrett" which was used in THE RHODES READER, and last and foremost, a chapter entitled "The Men Who Fought at Minden" which would have been 'Gene Rhodes at his hot-eyed best defending the name of Albert Bacon Fall and endeavoring to leave Fall's memory green and not besmirched.

The thought of what this book might have been and might have meant is enough to make any true-Rhodesian weep.

MOTION PICTURE BIBLIOGRAPHY

BRANSFORD IN ARCADIA — Eclair Film Corp., 8/10/1914.

No data on any remake.

DESIRE OF THE MOTH — Blue Bird Photoplays Inc., 9/25/- 1917, with Monroe Salsbury as the romantic lead, playing "Christopher Foy."

Remake by Universal, 4/25/1921, as *The Wallop*, starring Harry Carey as "John Wesley Pringle."

WEST IS WEST — Universal Film Mfg. Co., 11/12/1920, starring Harry Carey.

This used the book title but only pp. 191/273 of the book, being that portion devoted to the romance between "Dick Rainboldt" and "Judith Elliott". No data on any remake.

GOOD MEN AND TRUE — Robertson-Cole Pictures Corp., 11/- 12/1922, starring Harry Carey.

No remake data.

STEPSONS OF LIGHT — As *The Mysterious Witness;* Robertson-Cole, 6/24/1923.

No other data.

PASÓ POR AQUÍ — *As Four Faces West;* Harry Sherman Pictures, Inc., 5/16/1948 with Joel McCrea as *Ross McEwen,* Charles Bickford as *Pat Garrett.*

Publicity for the picture stressed Garrett's name and fame. "Poor Harry Sherman . . . I say 'poor' because Harry died, heart-broken, and I was very fond of him. Sherman spent many years making cheap westerns, very successfully, but finally in his old age he wanted to make a 'fine' western. He made it. I personally liked the picture very much . . . . . but the thing laid the biggest egg ever laid by any picture ever made in this business. It cost well over a million to make . . . I think the gross is still under $300,000. United Artists withdrew the picture from circulation, a thing that has happened only once or twice in all the history of Hollywood. Harry made the fatal mistake of doing an intelligent western with not one bit of action, not one shot fired, not even a fist-fight." [Frank Gruber to WHH, 1/11/1956.] The demand of television for material gave this picture a new lease on earning power which may, if past experiences are any criterion, go on forever in this medium.

THE PROUD SHERIFF — Sold to Baroda Productions Inc., 1955, presumably as a vehicle for Gary Cooper.

Not made as yet.

MAJOR REVIEW AND CRITICAL OPINION

It seems fortunate that this section can be headed with an appraisal of Rhodes written by Bernard DeVoto in November, 1933, for Brentano's *Book Chat* but not published therein. Houghton Mifflin Company distributed it as an advertising circular for THE TRUSTY KNAVES and many book pages used it in part as their review of this novel.

EUGENE MANLOVE RHODES

"It is my destiny to read all the books that are written about the West. I have been working at it for a long time: it must be twenty years since I first encountered Eugene Manlove Rhodes's novels. I thought then that they must be the finest ever written about that strange and violent and beautiful era in American life, the years of the cattle trade. Since that early recognition I have read all the others and I know now that I was right; his are the best. A very great many men have tried to put that time into books. Only a few of them knew what they were talking about, and of these few not all had the skill to match their knowledge. None of the best of them, I think, would question or resent the judgment that Gene Rhodes did the job better than they knew how.

"Belief is a strange thing. I have heard it urged against Mr. Rhodes that his novels were 'romantic' — and the term is explained as meaning that their stories are improbable. When will the profound understand that the West was an improbable country? They are not romantic to a Westerner. You realize his tremendous power of evoking that tremendous landscape. The effect is startling, it may be, even, improbable, but that is the landscape as it is and no one else has succeeded in reproducing it — and, as one who has tried, none too hopefully, to put that selfsame landscape into type, I may claim to recognize authenticity when I meet it. Well, the people and the stories of Gene Rhodes's books are no otherwise. These are the people who made that era, now over, and this is what they did. You will not hear one who knows the West calling Mr. Rhodes a romantic: you are more likely to hear him wondering why the romantic was not shot by this or that historic personage for recalling in print events that are a live topic to a good many and uncomfortable, I imagine, to more than a few. He is, of course, out of fashion, in that he prefers to write with wit and gusto and tenderness, qualities inappropriate to a cliché that currently makes the West the symbol of wasteland. But they are qualities of the man himself and of the time he records, the time he knows so intimately, and I prefer the probity that keeps them in his books.

"These are the qualities I have lingered on while reading *The Trusty Knaves* — its gusto, its tenderness and its wit. I could call attention to the care and precision of its structure, the workmanship that would have the paragraphers all one glad hymn of admiration if by some chance so much skill ever got into a novel about a sensitive young artist who came to feel bitter and took up the Revolution. Or I could mention the clear line of the story, the speed and ease with which it moves, the sureness of its telling, or the man's sheer style. But we Rhodesians take all that for granted, and this book is worthy to stand with its predecessors. I remember the first of Gene Rhodes's books I ever read, 'The Little Eohippus.' Twenty years between that book and this one — twenty years of a fine art, an honesty and clarity of recording and a sureness of interpretation that no one else who has ever treated his subject has equalled. One isn't moved to say that sort of thing about many American writers of today."

Pacific Pharos — This student publication at University of the Pacific carried the first literary mention, [9/25/1889] of Rhodes: "Rhodes is becoming distinguished as a rising poet." Following school custom, this tribute to Rhodes' agility or poetical ability, as desired, was unsigned.

Baltimore Sun — A long, unsigned review of *BRANSFORD IN ARCADIA* with two-column cut of the author, Feb. 22, 1914. Dubbing Rhodes "Ranchman and Disciple of Bret Harte", the review pays tribute to his intimate knowledge of the story's locale and prototypes. Fully half the review is a direct quote from the book, pp. 65/67, of Rhodes' homage to " . . . that hitherto unrecognized educator, Front de Boeuf" — being the Bull Durham-coupon books.

Becker, May Lamberton — in her column, The Readers Guide, *New York Herald-Tribune Books*, 7/12/1942, advises a reader who wanted to buy the best "Westerns" to get first the stories by Rhodes.

Bingham, Edwin R. — *Charles F. Lummis, Editor of the Southwest*, San Marino, The Huntington Library, 1955: as indexed. This very intelligent and detailed study of *Out West* and the man who made it devotes considerable space to Rhodes who was discovered, encouraged and initially instructed by Lummis. The biographical information on Rhodes was derived mainly from his wife's biography. The literary appraisal seems founded in DeVoto but the author, a faculty member at the University of Oregon, renders his own judgments. They are in Rhodes's favor but they are very fair in highlighting his early short-comings.

Of greatest interest to this bibliographer is Dr. Bingham's independent arrival at the conclusion that Rhodes used his fiction as a vehicle to make the social and literary East realize that the West and its people were not sub-humans living on the dark side of the moon.

Branch, E. Douglas — *The Cowboy and His Interpreters*, D. Appleton & Co., NY & London, 1926, p. 268: notes difference between writings of Rhodes, Andy Adams, Knibbs, Hough, Will James and Siringo and the pattern-fiction, bargain bookshelf novelists. Cites WEST IS WEST for his Rhodes selection.

W. H. C. *Boston Transcript*, 11/12/1938: review of THE HIRED MAN ETC. "Mr. Rhodes' stories . . . brought the essential details of Western life into sharp focus. Such a process, if writing mean anything at all, is literature. . . . That Rhodes wrote historical fiction as it should be written, that he was faithful to the people and the land that he knew best, that his characters were live creatures who walked and talked as men, that, in short, Rhodes wrote literature, meant nothing. He "typed" himself as the author of "Westerns." Nevertheless, there are devoted readers of Rhodes who have cleared the market of his books, particularly of the early titles."

Clark, Walter Van Tilburg — *New York Times* Book Review, 11/20/1949: a review of THE BEST NOVELS, etc., that is an appraisal of Rhodes' place in the literature of the American West and a succinct summary of his technical shortcomings. "And constantly there are the enormous landscapes — all so lovingly done that no other purveyor of the Western can even touch them." Considering Mr. Clark's own proficiency at evoking the face of the West in luminous prose, this is high praise indeed.

Cleaveland, Mrs. Agnes Morley — *Overland Monthly*, Dec., 1929, "Three Musketeers of Southwestern Fiction:" Rhodes, Dane Coolidge and John M. Oskison are the author's support for her title. "No chronicler of the life of the Southwest is superior to Gene Rhodes in honesty of portrayal, in style born of sincerity, nor in vision, which is the offspring of the deep-rooted love of the country of which he writes."

Crichton, Kyle — *Life*, Dec., 1933: a review of THE TRUSTY KNAVES. Despite what he did with Elfego Baca's life in *Law and Order Ltd.*, Crichton knew the real thing and Rhodes was it.

Cunningham, Eugene — *El Paso Times*, 12/7/30 - 10/6/35: the "Book Page" conducted by Cunningham in the Sunday edition is studded with notes, comments and asides about Rhodes. The most important appearing 7/8/1934; "Paso Por Aqui," a personal obituary for Rhodes which was the first use in print of this phrase to mark Rhodes' tenure on this cooling cinder and was used without the accent marks to give it present tense; and 12/30/1934; "Damocles Is Dead," to mark the demise of one of two cats Rhodes had used in his own preface to THE TRUSTY KNAVES.

Letter to Mrs. Helen Smith Ristvedt, 5/8/1937: " . . . he was so completely a part of our mountains and mesas that it is much like speaking of a peak, its genesis, to discuss him.

"If you knew this Southwestern country, there would (could) exist no smallest doubt in your mind concerning his locales. He was a poet-cowboy.

(Not a cowboy-poet) Words he loved for the color and shape and music of them. But he was cowboy in his original, whimsical fashion of expression, his indirectness of speech. . . . He called himself an incorrigible romantic. But his novels are realistic — in the same hazed and softened fashion that his beloved mountains are real when at dusk they rear as mauve and lavender silhouettes. . . . Nothing is hurried; nothing twisted for the sake of an effect. There is spaciousness everywhere in his pages; more than color, even, they possess the fine dignity of leisurely thought. His cowboys come jogging across great distances. They watch a peak for sixty, a hundred, miles. They think about it and slowly, surely, forge an unforgettable phrase that perfectly describes it.

He wrote inimitably of the Southwest and its people . . . and wrote inimitably because (more than any other of the writing guild) Gene Rhodes was spokesman for his own kind, the cowboy, the Southwesterner. . . . "

—— *New Mexico Magazine*, Dec., 1938: ostensibly a review of THE HIRED MAN ON HORSEBACK. Actually, this long essay is about Rhodes, as Man and Writer, by a master craftsman in the same field who is, also, a profound student of *belles lettres* and who knew Rhodes, as Man and Writer.

—— "Better Westerns" in *The Craft of Novel Writing*, edited by A. S. Burack, Boston, 1942: the essay covers pp. 171/181 and was included in *The Writer's Handbook*, edited by Burack, Boston, 1953. Pages 178/181 are an appreciation of Rhodes as the "Big Old He" of Western novelists.

Cuppy, Will — *New York Herald-Tribune*, BOOKS, 11/12/1933, p. 27: review of THE TRUSTY KNAVES; 9/22/1934, p. 14: review of BEYOND THE THE DESERT. Cuppy conducted a "Mystery and Adventure Page." That Rhodes' books appeared there, in face of the competition, is the point to be considered as is Cuppy's summation: ". . . superior historical-cowboy romances."

Davidson, Levette J. — *Western Humanities Review*, Spring, 1951, "The Literature of Western America." This examination of the virgins-villians-and-varmints *genre* by a distinguished folklorist and teacher of English Literature notes ". . . Eugene Manlove Rhodes' *Saturday Evening Post* novelettes — now undergoing belated critical acclaim."

DeVoto, Bernard — *The Saturday Review of Literature*, 10/17/1936, "Horizon Land - I," this editorial was the first major appreciation of Rhodes to reach any body of informed thought. Another editorial, 4/24/1937; "Horizon Land-II" had this to say: "Thirty years of cheap fiction about cowboys, rustlers, evil sheriffs, roundups, stampedes, six guns and branding irons have created an inertia which serious literature finds it hard to overcome. Having produced Eugene Manlove Rhodes it needed another quarter century to produce Mr. Conrad Richter."

—— "Eugene Manlove Rhodes," an essay written for Brentano's *Book Chat* but not published. Houghton, Mifflin used it as advertising for THE TRUSTY KNAVES, and many reviewers simply quoted in whole or part for their review of this book. Cf. El Paso *Times*, 12/31/1933; San Diego *Union*, 1/28/1934.

—— "The Novelist of the Cattle Kingdom," as the Introduction to THE HIRED MAN ON HORSEBACK, Boston, 1938. Expanded and refined from the previous material, this is the most literate study of Rhodes yet written. It expresses the summation " . . . the only fiction of the cattle kingdom which approaches a level that it is intelligent to call art."

—— *Harper's Magazine*, Dec., 1954, "Phaethon on Gunsmoke Trail": an essay on the Western story in the author's department, "The Easy Chair." After twenty-plus years since his first salvo, Devoto still is a Rhodesian, despite Richter's, *The Sea of Grass*, and Clark's, *The Ox-Bow Incident*.

—— *Harper's Magazine*, Dec., 1955, "Birth of an Art": an essay on Owen Wister, his literary origins and his place in spawning the "western" story in "The Easy Chair." Speaking of *The Virginian*, he says: "The cowboy story has seldom produced anything as good; apart from Gene Rhodes, it has not even tried to do anything different."

Dobie, J. Frank and Rogers, Jno. W. — *Finding Literature on the Texas Plains*, Dallas, 1931, p. 50: "Eugene Manlove Rhodes has written a half-dozen novels far superior to the false, feeble and flatulent 'westerns' with which they must perforce compete. . . . Mr. Rhodes has a natural gayety that is very pleasing." WEST IS WEST, STEPSONS OF LIGHT, GOOD MEN AND TRUE are mentioned by name.

Dobie, J. Frank — *On the Open Range*, Dallas, 1931; reprint, Banks, Upshaw & Co., 1940, p. 299.

—— *Southwest Review*, Spring, 1934; review of THE TRUSTY KNAVES. ". . . he has reported the Old West aright, and has a passionate loyalty to it, plus the power of expression . . . . only O. Henry and Alfred Henry Lewis among fictionists of the West can vie with him in the grace of literary allusion."

—— *Southwest Review*, January, 1939: review of THE HIRED MAN ON HORSEBACK, which was a crystallization of Dobie's feelings about Rhodes and his work.

"Rhodes was an artist in the painful care he gave to structure, the whole plot — always dominant in his novels — the niceties of character, and the wit of conversation. His range characters are as neat and apt in literary allusion as Agnes Repplier herself; yet not one sacrifices fidelity to his own flavor of speech in order to say a good thing. . . . He was not a world compeller. He was more bighearted than great. Nevertheless, I think their sheer gayety will make some of his stories live a long time. Rhodes fulfills the requirements laid down by Willkie Collins for story-telling; 'Make 'em laugh, make 'em cry, make 'em wait.' He was not many-sided or 'infinitely various.' He had but one string to his fiddle, but he played it with infinite variations and got tunes out of it honest and old and plain like the ballads and they 'danced like a bit o'the sun.' This is something rare in American literature. It is very precious.

" . . . His own heard him gladly and his own received him. No man who has anything to say could ask for a higher reward."

—— *Apache Goldand Yaqui Silver*, Boston, 1939; reprints a long extract from STEPSONS OF LIGHT, pp. 82/86.

—— *The Longhorns*, Boston, 1941, p. 254: cites Ross McEwen's steer-riding from PASÓ POR AQUÍ and Rhodes' inscription in Eugene Cunningham's copy of the book about the incident as Rhodes had done it personally.

——*Guide to Life and Literature of the Southwest,* Univ. Texas Press, 1942, p. 67; rev. ed., S.M.U. Press, 1952, p. 115: in the ten years between editions, Don Pancho revised his opinion of Rhodes. Deletions from the original are shown below in brackets; changes in the revised version are italicized:

"Gene Rhodes had the 'right tune.' He achieved a style that [is truly literary.] *can be called literary.* Perhaps Pasó Por Aquí will endure as his masterpiece. Rhodes had an intense loyalty to his land and people; he was as gay, gallant and witty as he was earnest. More than [any other] *most* Western writers Rhodes was conscious of art. He had the common touch and also he was a writer for writing men. The elements [of nobility and gayety,] of simplicity and the right kind of sophistication, always with generosity and with an unflagging zeal for the rights of [all] human beings were [strangely] mixed in him. The reach of any ample-natured man exceeds his grasp. Rhodes was ample-natured, but he cannot be classed as great because his grasp was too often disporportionately short of the long reach. *His fiction becomes increasingly dated."*

—— "My Salute to Gene Rhodes," in THE LITTLE WORLD WADDIES, El Paso, 1946: see printing history under book title herein.

—— *A Texas Cowboy,* New York, 1950: in his Notes to this edition of Siringo's book, Dobie quotes Rhodes on Siringo and uses the Bull Durham coupon books anecdote from BRANSFORD IN ARCADIA.

Dykes, Jeff C. — *Billy the Kid, The Bibliography of a Legend,* Albuquerque, 1952, as indexed: lists various Rhodes' items pertaining to *alias Bonney* and Pat Garrett.

Terms Rhodes' "In Defense of Pat Garrett" . . . "masterful."

—— "High Spots of Western Fiction: 1902-1952," *The Brand Book,* Chicago Westerners, Sept., 1955: pp. 49-51, 53-55.

One of the most sapient bibliophiles of the entire Western scene includes Rhodes in his "High Spots" and dubs him " . . . my favorite cow country novelist for more than forty years." Cites GOOD MEN AND TRUE, BRANSFORD IN ARCADIA, WEST IS WEST, and THE TRUSTY KNAVES as his selections of Rhodes's best.

Fergusson, Erna — *New Mexico Quarterly,* Spring, 1950, pp. 112/113, "Western Nostalgia:" a review of THE BEST NOVELS etc.

" . . . Much of it is nostalgia, though it may be that when the young and brash critics who do not like Rhodes' style or his point of view have been forgotten Gene, like Stevenson, will be revived as a writer of good, racy and characteristic prose.

"One might take exception to Dobie's statement that Rhodes' characters' 'talk is uniformly natural.' Frank Dobie has known more cowboys than I have and it may be that they uniformly talk like this: rounded periods, sparkling with whimsicalities, heavily larded with classical allusions and apt Biblical and Shakespearean quotations. But somehow I doubt it. . . . I suspect they are all Gene Rhodes . . . who loved the vernacular and used it as well as he used the classical speech. But who, whatever he did, did it like a literary man.

"So were his plots literary, intricately contrived. Inconceivable that such things could have happened. But they were fun to read, as any lover of stories

61

would have to admit. They are, in addition, unfailingly true to the scene in which they are laid. . . . Most of all, his tales are true with the truth-to-type of a man who writes of life not as it was or even as he knew it to be, but as a man of his generation would speak of people not present — with gentle judiciousness. Only his villains are presented with some rancor, but amused rancor and in the sure knowledge that they will be downed in the end when the knightly hero gets the delicate heroine, whose hair is soft and misty even in a sandstorm and whose hands are always small. No wonder *Saturday Evening Post* readers loved Gene devotedly for a whole generation.

This is a volume to have at hand for escape reading or to put on the guest-room table."

—— *New Mexico*: *A Pageant of Three Peoples*, New York, 1952: chapter "Artist Discoverers."

Miss Fergusson does not mention Rhodes in this chapter and says: "Even writers of the Westerns truest to detail and talk are often newcomers who saw cowboys at first hand."

Miss Fergusson's comments are made more interesting by the fact that she and her brother, fellow-novelist Harvey Fergusson, are the children of Harvey Butler Fergusson who came to New Mexico in 1882 and had a long, stirring and distinguished life there until his death in 1915. H. B. Fergusson, among other things, was associated with Albert Bacon Fall in the defense of Oliver Lee and Jim Gililland for the alleged murders of Colonel A. J. Fountain and his son, Henry.

Ford, Thomas F. — *Los Angeles Times*, 5/29/1927: review of ONCE IN THE SADDLE.

" . . . Here then are two stories that breathe the very spirit of the West. . . . the West that Gene Rhodes knows so well and loves so dearly, and that because of that knowledge and that love he has been able to give a place in Literature."

Ford, long-time Literary Editor of the *Times*, had been a friend of Rhodes in the Arroyo Seco years.

Frantz, Joe B. and Choate, Julian E. Jr. — *The American Cowboy, The Myth and the Reality*, Norman, 1955; as indexed.

The authors cite DeVoto and Dobie, mainly, in giving Rhodes a niche in the ranks of fictioneers about the Cattle Kingdom; they disagree with Dobie's view that B. M. Bower's novels were almost as good as were Rhodes's.

They say, also: "Critics are divided on just how good Rhodes was. They agree he was a rare craftsman, but they also think he had more craft than heart."

Regardless of this opinion and of DeVoto's expression in 1933, a vigorous dissent to Rhodes's craftsmanship must be registered. What lifts Rhodes out of the ruck is his heart, his subjective recall of the days, ways, people and places of his youth.

The further statement is made in this compendium that: "Rhodes also fell short in neglecting to consider the impelling power which the color and romance of the myths and legends of the cowboy hold over the imagination of the American folk. The realism of *Moby Dick* may contribute to that novel's value, but its mysticism and symbolism have made it great. And it is here that Rhodes fell down, that, in fact, the whole realm of cowboy fiction falls down, for the fiction of the frontier days won't be truly accepted as classic unless and until the archetypal myths are woven into the story, for they are a part of the American folk mind."

It is not a pleasant task to point out that considering Rhodes's point in time, he was one of the creators of the popular mythology, though he could not stem its distortion. Neither is it pleasant to point out that Messers. Frantz and Choate apparently cannot recognize the archetypal myths they seek unless the same come to them cloaked in the conventional habiliments purveyed by the literary haberdashers of the "western."

Gould, Charles N. — *The Oklahoman*, [Oklahoma City] 3/3/1935: a review of THE PROUD SHERIFF.

Interesting chiefly because it uses so very little from Gould's long, correspondence-friendship with Rhodes.

Gruber, Frank — "Riding the Rim," *The Roundup*, Jan., 1956, p. 10.

In this monthly organ of the Western Writers of America, Mr. Gruber discussed the origins and practitioners of the "western." Speaking of Zane Grey and the early period Grey represented, he said: "Eugene Manlove Rhodes, today the darling of a small western 'literary' clique, was turning out some rather dull western prose."

Coming from one of the most highly successful technicians and craftsmen in the field, this comment is more eloquent as to Rhodes's technique and craft than any other possible comment could be.

Hart, James D. — *The Oxford Companion to American Literature*, Oxford Univ. Press, 1941, p. 636:

" . . . his faithful depiction of the contemporary background and characters and the quality of his prose keep his work from the sentimentality and cheap melodrama of the usual tales of cowboy adventure."

Henderson, Alice C. — *Publisher's Weekly*, 6/11/1927, pp. 2247/2248: "A Santa Fe Bookshelf."

Mentions Rhodes' enthusiastic support of Southwestern work and his telephoning her daily from Tesuque not to forget Raine, Coolidge, Spearman, etc. In her list, "Novels and Stories of New Mexican Life," five of the twenty-three entries are Rhodes, all of his books to-date with the exception of BRANSFORD IN ARCADIA.

—— *New Mexico, A Guide to the Colorful State*, Hastings House, 1940; completely rev. ed., 1953, p. 134: chapter on "Literature."

"Swift-moving and keen with philosophic wit, his books will outlive the rank and file of mere 'westerns' . . . all authentic tales of the veritable soil and soul of the New Mexican cattle range."

Henry, Stuart — *Conquering Our Great American Plains*, New York, 1930, Appendix. To be read only with knowledge of Rhodes' part in debating Henry's review of Emerson Hough's posthumous novel, *North of 36*, for which see A BAR CROSS MAN.

Hutchinson, W. H. — *Western Humanities Review*, January, 1949, "The Western

63

Story as Literature:" an opinionated essay by a man who knew more then than he does now.

—— *San Francisco Chronicle*, 11/20/1949: review of THE BEST NOVELS etc.

Most subjective, most uncritical.

—— *Huntington Library Quarterly*, August, 1953, "Virgins, Villains and Varmints:" essay on the "Western story" as literature.

Prose version of the author's oral seminar on the subject. Manages to give Rhodes high-rank with nods towards Owen Wister, Andy Adams, Stewart Edward White, Eugene Cunningham, Alan LeMay and Harry Sinclair Drago. Used as Introduction, expanded, in THE RHODES READER.

Izzard, Wes — *Amarillo* [Texas] *Sunday News-Globe*, 7/4/1948:

Using his column, "From the Editor's Desk," as his vehicle, Wes Izzard wrote a long letter to the Univ. of New Mexico Press asking them, in essence, why they did not keep Rhodes' books in print as a public service. Ranks Rhodes with Bret Harte and Owen Wister and stacks several of Rhodes' stories against Mark Twain's classic about The Jumping Frog.

Jackson, Joseph Henry. — *Saturday Review of Literature*, 10/15/1938: a review of THE HIRED MAN ON HORSEBACK.

—— *San Francisco Chronicle*, 10/15/1938: review of same book as above, slightly different; 11/16/1947 and 1/24/1947, mention, then review of THE LITTLE WORLD WADDIES. " . . . he wrote about the Southwest, the cattle country, the desert, the mountains. But this did not make him a horse-opera man, not by a very long shot indeed. Rhodes was a great deal more than that. His work was shot through with humor, with wit, with literary allusion. He wrote a prose that was simple, clear, sharp, exact. In short, Eugene Manlove Rhodes was a very good writer."

James, George Wharton — *New Mexico* — *The Land of the Delight Makers*, Boston, 1920, pp. 365/366: mention, *en passant*, by the man who succeeded C. F. Lummis as editor of *Out West*.

Julian, Hurst — *Saturday Review of Literature*, 7/13/1940, pp. 13/15, "The Real Fiction in Western Stories:"

Uses Rhodes as the exception that proves his premise: " . . . authors of western stories know nothing about the subject."

Some inexpensive amusement can be had by picking flaws in Mr. Julian's own statements.

K. C. K. — *Christian Science Monitor*, 10/14/1938: review of THE HIRED MAN etc., titled "Cyrano in Chaps."

" . . . it was in the East that he wrote his best works — works which stand literally alone in the literature of the West: . . . perfect compounds of realism and romance. His stories run in a pattern. His sympathies were ever with the underdog, the victim of circumstances, the 'good-bad' man, and he delighted in meting out justice to the vain, to proud sheriffs and political bosses and corrupt financiers while his ladies were ideals of chivalry. But — it is this very attitude that makes him one of the true *Vates* of the West.

"This sensitive understanding, plus the artistry of his words — there was something of the Celtic magic in his prose, far more poetical than his verse —

and the fact that he was a splendid storyteller, entitle him to a place among the classics."

Kahler, Hugh McNair — Letter to W. H. H., 12/18/1952: "The future has a right to know everything that can be known about him and about the things and the works that made him great."

As both successful writer and most competent editor, *Ladies Home Journal*, Hugh Kahler knows whereof he speaks.

Keleher, Julia — *New Mexico Quarterly*, August, 1936: in her department, "Los Paisanos."

"It is generally conceded by representative Southwestern admirers of Mr. [Conrad] Richter, that the place left vacant by the late Eugene Manlove Rhodes in the literary world will be filled by this prolific author, and the reputation which he has already achieved warrants this judgment."

Brief mentions of Rhodes and his various works appear in this department of the *Quarterly* while conducted by Miss Keleher over the next ten years. On the faculty of New Mexico University and a sister of Wm. A. Keleher, of Albuquerque, Miss Keleher had both a professional and a personal interest in Rhodes.

King, Frank M. — *Western Livestock Journal*, 11/30/1933: review of THE TRUSTY KNAVES.

Literarily valueless but valid as evidence of Rhodes' accurate portrayal of scene and character.

In his column "Mavericks," in this journal, King made numerous references to and mentions of Rhodes until his death.

Kitchen, Paul — Letter to W. H. H., November, 1952: "He was one of the most deliberately conscious stylists in American letters, and in his *genre* an absolute anomaly."

Interesting comment by an informed layman, reader, bibliophile and friend of Vincent Starret.

Knibbs, Henry H. — *Saddle Songs*, Boston & New York, 1922: dedicated to Rhodes.

Lake, Stuart N. — San Diego *Union*, 10/7/1934: review of BEYOND THE DESERT; 2/24/1935: review of *The Proud Sheriff*; 10/23/1938: review of THE HIRED MAN, etc.

The essence of Lake's feelings is taken from his review of 2/24/1935: "Gene Rhodes was a born story-teller, a yarn-spinner for the sake of the yarn itself who had few peers. And, had the term 'western' not accumulated more or less opprobium through the efforts of slovenly commentators to classify novels by settings rather than by worth, he would have been accorded during his lifetime unquestionably the niche in the fiction hall of fame to which the sound critics and the superficial ones, as well, lifted him . . . in the weeks immediately following his death."

Lindemann, Lauris H. — *Frontier and Midland*, Winter, 1934/5: review of BEYOND THE DESERT; Summer, 1935; review of the THE PROUD SHERIFF.

The comment is from the latter review in which he keynotes from Rhodes' introductory essay to THE TRUSTY KNAVES: " ' I claim for these men of whom I write . . . a joyous and loving heart, a decent respect for others and for themselves, and courage enough to master fear.' with Rhodes, the virtues of the West were as casual as that; and he never set to paper a more disregarded truth. All his books have the factual authenticity of THE PROUD SHERIFF, the same subtle permeation of his love for the country, the same laconic expression and miraculous characterization. . . . His death left a real gap in the ranks of truly Western writers of fiction."

Lummis, C. F. — *Mesa, Canyon and Pueblo*, Century 1925, pp. 494/495: the only mention that Rhodes cherished prior to Webb's notice of him in *The Great Plains*.

"Of the vivid but fast-disappearing Romance of the Cowboy, the Open Range, and The Long Trail . . . incomparably the best descriptions are by Emerson Hough, and in fiction by Eugene Manlove Rhodes."

Morley, Sylvanus G. — *New Mexico Quarterly*, Autumn, 1946, pp. 255 *passim*, p. 259: "Cowboy and Gaucho Fiction."

"Eugene Manlove Rhodes deserves a special word . . . no man worked harder over his style. The result of such severe self-criticism is one of the most solid and distinguished styles written by any North American novelist. I would call Rhodes a first-rate writer of third-rate novels, for their sentences, humor, accuracy and color are as admirable as their characters are distorted and impossible."

Letter to W. H. H.: "I have a particular affection for that born stylist and upstanding man."

Morley, on the faculty of the University of California at Berkeley, profound student of Hispanic-American civilization, was a cousin of Mrs. Agnes Morley Cleaveland.

Pearce, T. M. — *New Mexico Quarterly*, November, 1938: review of THE HIRED MAN etc.

"Rhodes . . . had the insight into the sterling sympathies, loyalties, courage and humor that held society together in the wide flung empire of range and ranches covering most of the western mountains and prairies. His people live objective lives. They settle the problems of right and wrong without psycho-analyzing the background of the criminal or placing the charge on his environment. This world which Rhodes knew, a world that demanded of men a joyous and a loving heart, a decent respect for others and courage enough to master fear, makes a poor splice with the sophisticated literary society of today."

Pearce, T. M.; Major, Mabel; Smith, Rebecca — *Southwest Heritage*, Albuquerque, 1938; rev. ed. 1948; pp. 88/89: calls Rhodes "Probably the most significant of the realistic romancers of the plains. . . ."

Powell, Lawrence Clark — *Heart of the Southwest*, Dawson's Book Shop, Los Angeles, 1955: items 88, 89, 90 in this selective bibliography are Rhodesian.

The Librarian of the University of California at Los Angeles used the chief criterion of "fidelity to the characteristics of this region, its landscape and weather, its people and lore." In the 119 items he measured by this yardstick, he chose three of the early Rhodes; "THE DESIRE OF THE MOTH, ONCE IN THE SADDLE and WEST IS WEST. He calls Rhodes: ". . . the most literary and humanistic cowboy writer of them all."

—— *The Last Frontiersman*, UCLA Library, 1957: this catalog of an exhibit selected by Powell cites THE BEST NOVELS, etc.

—— *Arizona Highways*, March, 1958: More Powell on the literature of the Southwest and its practitioners including Rhodes.

Larry Powell's opinions are worth having — and hearing. *Es Verdad!*

Richter, Conrad — *New Mexico Quarterly*, May 1934, pp. 144/145: joint review of PEÑALOSA AND THE TRUSTY KNAVES.

"Here are two prints of the same hand left for our comparison sixteen years apart in the white strata of the Papyrus Age. The first, firmly compressed, laid down in the historical manner and glistening with brilliant hardness, might be the hand of any one of a good many contemporary artists. But there is no mistaking the identity of the second. The latter is unpretentious. There is no grand gesture or finger pointing at some magnificant scene, and yet of all the teeming millions who can take their pen in hand, I doubt the existence of another human being who could have done it.

"Like Joseph Conrad, there is only one Eugene Manlove Rhodes and no one remotely resembling him. . . . Rhodes' robust vigor and contrasting gentleness, his gusto, his long, firsthand intimacy with his land and its people, his raciness, his wit and sardonic humor, his subtlety and its strange bedfellow, a recurring sense of beauty; perhaps most of all, his nonconformity and his delight in strewing literary gems in the most unexpected of places are talents for which the reading world will wait a long time before being found again in the same mortal combination.

"Anyone who comes to Rhodes expecting the traditional Western story is bound to stub his toe severely, and in my mind I can see Gene Rhodes' eyes twinkling at the puzzled face of such a reader. But the searcher for personality on the printed page, the man who loves boundless, highly-flavored life wherever he finds it, who has learned from reality not to be surprised to find even the most primitive society for the most part kind and strong, shrewd and tremendously human whether on Hudson's pampas, in Aksakoff's old Russia, in Barrie's Thrums, or on Rassul Galwan's Tibetan plateau — such a reader will come on Rhodes with unquenchable delight. . . ."

Schriftgiesser, Karl — *Newsweek*, 11/7/1949, pp. 92/95, "The Real Thing"; review of THE BEST NOVELS etc., by the magazine's Book Editor, and an evident Rhodesian:

". . . Why Rhodes's work is not better known is one of the mysteries of American literature. Some of his short stories are masterpieces; some of his novels approach greatness and in part achieve it. All of his work summons up with extraordinary clarity the ranch and town life of the Southwest . . . . Rhodes's plots are weakened by too great a straining for surprise and novelty; his conversations are sometimes mannered and artificial, and his humor is occasionally dated and exaggerated. But a love for his native section glows through his works with a genuine ardor. . . ."

Shippey, Lee — Los Angeles *Times*, various dates as shown; from Shippey's column "The Lee Side O'LA:"

—— 5/17/1931: long, 2 col.x12 appreciation of Rhodes ". . . something of the humor of Bret Harte, something of the art of Conrad, and the genuine knowledge of the West of Walt Coburn. . . . Rhodes fans are like O'Henry fans or Conrad fans — they have a sort of worship for him."

—— 12/29/1933: contains an anecdote about Gene and mentions issuance of THE TRUSTY KNAVES, a piece inspired by Harrison Leussler who fed Shippey the material.

—— 7/5/1934: personal obituary by Shippey with a discussion of various writers on whom Rhodes' mantle would descend. Walt Coburn and W. C. Tuttle were possibilities but had written too much pulp material; the same trap, writing as a business, had snared H. Bedford Jones and Wm. Mac L. Raine. Zane Grey's place was not Rhodes'. H. H. Knibbs was a strong contender but Shippey thought Hal G. Evarts or Alan LeMay the most likely successors.

—— 10/21/1938: a boost for the Eugene Manlove Rhodes Memorial Association and a boost for THE HIRED MAN etc; more Leussler-fed material.

SONNICHSEN, C. L. — *Tularosa, Last of the West;* to be published in 1959 by Devin-Adair; pagination of chapter on Rhodes, "Bard of the Tularosa," unknown at this writing.

From his vantage point at Texas Western College in El Paso, Professor Sonnichsen has unearthed several fresh anecdotes about Rhodes to leaven the dough of his other citations. Beyond these things, he makes a fair appraisal of Rhodes in relation to his country and his people and his writings about them. This particular Rhodes Scholar cannot agree in any way with the Sonnichsenion theory that Rhodes' novel, COPPER STREAK TRAIL, contains a wayward apology for the alleged involvement of Oliver Lee in the Fountain disappearance.

Spiller, Thorp, Johnson, Canby — *Literary History of the United States,* New York, 1948, Vol. II, p. 872: places Andy Adams, Alfred Henry Lewis and Owen Wister, in ascending order, as those who made the cowboy respectable enough for serious literature.

"Though their lead has been followed since by Eugene Manlove Rhodes and others, their performance has not yet been bettered."

Starrett, Vincent — *Books and Bipeds,* Argus, New York, 1947, pp. 84/86: discusses Rhodes and the Bull Durham-coupon books.

—— *Chicago Sunday Tribune,* 11/13/1949, "Boks Alive": review of THE BEST NOVELS etc.

"I suppose it is because Rhodes wrote 'westerns' that he is ignored by the historians; but it is a capital mistake to think of him as merely one of the company of Zane Grey and B. M. Bower — whose lesser entertainments I do not mean to disparage. Gene Rhodes was a fine prose artist, a magnificent story-teller, a humorist of noble stature; and, believe me, he is an authentic American classic. . . . Sure, he was a romantic, and a peculiarly sentimental one at times. His stories are often fairly sticky and old fashioned; but there will be time enough to deny him a place among the good writers of America when Scott and Stevenson, say, are refused a position in English letters. I am sorry that I have no time to develop the analogy."

Tully, Jim — *Story World,* October, 1923, "Writers I Have Known": in the course of his name-dropping, Tully acknowledges Rhodes' assistance in getting him started; says Rhodes is greater than anything he has written and nominates him to write the great classic of the American West.

Vaden, Clay — *New Mexico Quarterly*, May, 1935: review of THE PROUD SHERIFF by the editor of the *Catron County News*, Quemado, New Mexico.

"Once again he proved that he was the greatest writer of Western tales for he demonstrates beyond a doubt that he knew his country and its people and drew most of his characters from life and selected events in this fast moving action story which actually occurred. . . .

"Gene Rhodes has passed on . . . but he is still loved and his memory cherished in the hearts of his loyal friends who feel that his Spirit — the man's real self — laughs courageously at you through the unusual words of his self-written epitaph.

'Now hushed at last the murmur of his mirth,
Here he lies quiet in the quiet earth.
— When the last trumpet sounds on land and sea
He will arise then, chatting cheerfully,
And, blandly interrupting Gabriel,
He will go sauntering down the road to hell.
He will pause loitering at the infernal gate,
Advising Satan on affairs of state,
Complaining loudly that the roads are bad
And bragging what a jolly grave he had!' "

Van Doren, Carl — *The American Novel*, Macmillan, rev. and enlarged edition, 1940, pp. 362 and 382: mentions Rhodes as a cowboy writer of westerns — the best ones but still westerns. " . . . the most truthful and the least conventional."

The first edition of this work, Macmillan, 1921, carried no mention of Rhodes.

Vestal, Stanley [*W. S. Campbell*] — *The Book Lover's Southwest*, Norman, 1955: as indexed:

Rhodes thought highly of Stanley Vestal's work, encouraging him with one long letter which Vestal cherished. In his comments in this highly personalized bibliography, Vestal shows a reciprocal feeling which is not subjective.

Wagenknecht, Edward — *Chicago Sunday Tribune*, 6/27/1949; review of THE BEST NOVELS etc from advance sheets:

"Eugene Manlove Rhodes is one of the few writers of 'westerns' who ever has been taken seriously by the literati. This is a considerable achievement.

"The story classifications, however, do not matter very much, for the novels tend to be rather short and the short stories rather long, and none of them is a short story in the technical sense.

"You do not have to be interested in cowboys to read Rhodes with enjoyment; you only need to be interested in good fiction. Though he used all the 'properties' of Buffalo Bill, Broncho Billy and Wm. S. Hart, he was no more a 'cowboy writer' than Conrad was a 'Malay writer' or than Marian Anderson is a 'Negro singer.' He was a writer — a writer with style, integrity, distinction, and a generally unimpeachable sense of values. Though he was not so great as Conrad, his attitude toward the material which life brought him was not unlike the great Pole's. . . . "

Walker, Stanley — *New York Herald-Tribune*, 10/16/1938, "Books," p. 5; review of THE HIRED MAN etc., half-page with photograph:

Dubbing Rhodes "The Best 'Western' Writer of Them All," Walker quotes extensively from DeVoto's Introduction to the book. His own comments are germane: " . . . Rhodes was a remarkable man, wild, self-taught, uncompromising and thoroughly genuine. . . . if the publication of this biography can revive interest in the works of that hard-bitten master of simplicity, so much the better for literature. . . . The man, to lovers of the authentic West, will be remembered for a long time. His West was not the West of gaudy circus pageantry, but a way of life in which he had grown up. He told of it honestly in stories that have the mark of the expert craftsman. . . . "

Walsh, Maurice — *Twentieth Century Authors*, Wilson, New York, 1942, p. 1471; in his own biographical sketch therein:

"Favorite book: *West Is West* and all other stories by Eugene Manlove Rhodes, because he writes true Romance, which is the ideal made real, not the real made ideal."

Webb, Walter P. — *The Great Plains*, Ginn and Co., New York, 1931, pp. 463/464; Chapter X herein is devoted to "The Literature of the Great Plains and About the Great Plains;" Webb ranks Rhodes next to Andy Adams in fidelity to fact:

" . . . Like Adams, Rhodes has failed of deserved recognition, largely because he made his stories true to life in the cattle country rather than to the Eastern notions of what life there ought to be. His failure to win popular favor is probably attributable in part also to a packed style and the use of intricate plots which make his narratives hard to follow. He is inclined to compliment his readers by assuming considerable intellectual prowess on their part, in this respect bearing some resemblance to Joseph Conrad. Rhodes differs from Adams and Hough in that he deals with incidents and personalities rather than with historical events. His idea of the character and quality of the cowboy was expressed as follows: 'If Genghis Khan, Alexander, Napoleon and a cowboy were out together, there would be just four men in camp.' Among cowboys Rhodes sees no masters and no servants."

Rhodes felt that this "lyrical praise" of him by Webb barred him from reviewing Webb's book in which it appeared.

Wister, Owen — A comment on Rhodes to Theodore Roosevelt, paraphrased to W. H. H. by Arthur F. Martin: "He is the most honest and factual writer of the West and its men I ever knew."

Rhodes on Wister: "Owen Wister — apart from his stories — reminds me of a second lieutenant."

Woodburn, John — *The New Republic*, 12/12/1949, p. 28; review of THE BEST NOVELS etc.:

" . . . He had been a part of the Old West, had loved and understood it, and had written of it honorably, with gusto and sensitivity. He died before Autry climbed back in the saddle again and before, to a generation of moppets crouched over radios, the slam of a Smith & Wesson had become associated with the sound of breakfast food being shot from guns.

" . . . He wrote of the literate cowboy which is another way of saying he wrote of himself. This valuable collection . . . restores to dignity and to its original fresh, raw colors, a western way of life now too often relegated to the Catskill cowboy and the Reno gaucho. One cannot read . . . any of these exuberant, sad and sensitive tales without realizing that this neglected writer is the best who ever wrote on the region."

Woolford, Withers — *New Mexico Magazine*, December, 1933; review of THE TRUSTY KNAVES.

"When . . . writes Westerns they are almost as good history as they are fiction. No other writer of the Old West has found the full color of the people or the flavor of a world in the making as he has.

"Many others claiming to write Westerns manage to get in more action, but it is the action of fiction rather than of living and breathing people. Rhodes may not have so many broncos slithering down precipitous cliffs or so many 'six guns spewing leaden death.' He peoples his pages with the men who tamed the wild country that was a few years ago the West. . . .

"The story is more an historical novel in a setting that is as foreign to the ordinary historical romance as Rhodes is to the ordinary writer of Westerns. . . . "

—— *New Mexico Magazine*, February, 1934: review of PEÑALOSA.

" . . . In her Introduction to the volume, Alice Corbin says: 'One need know Rhodes only through his stories to understand why this rusty sword of Spanish days is unsheathed for the man who forfeited glory in behalf of a kind priest and a little brown child in Santa Fé centuries ago.'"

BIBLIOGRAPHER'S NOTES

Most interesting among the foregoing is the comparison of Rhodes to Joseph Conrad by a diversity of peoples and viewpoints.

Interesting, too, is the omission of any reference to Rhodes, but not to his apparent *genre*, by the following students of both history and literature: Joseph Warren Beach, *American Fiction, 1920-1940*, N. Y., 1941; Percy H. Boynton, *The Rediscovery of the Frontier*, Chicago, 1931, *Literature and American Life*, 1936; and *America in Contemporary Fiction*, Chicago, 1940; Lucy Lockwood Hazard, *The Frontier in American Literature*, N. Y., 1927; Harry Hartwick, *Foreground of American Fiction*, N. Y., 1934; Fred B. Millett, *Contemporary American Authors*, N. Y., 1940; Arthur Hobson Quinn, *American Fiction*, N. Y., 1936.

The importance of popular periodicals as Rhodes' major fiction outlet, coupled with the small number and small sales of his first books, is reflected in *Men Who Make Our Novels*, by George Gordon, Moffatt Yard & Co., N. Y., 1919.

Owen Wister, Stewart Edward White, Emerson Hough, Harold Bell Wright, Rex Ellingwood Beach and Zane Grey are among those informally discussed by Mr. Gordon. Rhodes is not mentioned.

Even as biographers of John Charles Fremont fall inevitably under the spell of his wife, so did those who knew Rhodes, either personally or through correspondence, fall under the spell of the Man, himself. Those perceptive writers, critics and readers who did not know Rhodes felt the permeating flavor of the Man in all his prose and verse. Thus, in appraisals, Man and Work are indivisible as they were in life and this is no mean tribute to the enduring worth of what he wrote.

ASSOCIATION ITEMS

Alamogordo [NM] *Daily News* — Article, 6/15/1956; on plans to make a local Rhodes shrine out of a replica of his old house there. [Each year, this newspaper carries news stories and features about the annual pilgrimage to Rhodes' grave in the San Andrés Range. These have not been cited in detail for reasons of space and value]

Americana Annual — Edition of 1935, p. 612: carries obituary sketch with date of death in error.

Badger, Mrs. Stanwood — *Los Angeles Sunday Times,* 7/12/1931: Feature Story and uncritical appreciation by one of his Los Angeles friends. Contains personal remembrances of Rhodes when he lived in the Arroyo Seco and some reminiscences about Rhodes by Robert Martin.

Bailey, Harry H. — *When New Mexico Was Young,* Las Cruces, 1948: book printing of Bailey's articles in the *Las Cruces Citizen,* 1946 et. seq. Contains several human-interest anecdotes by this boyhood friend and minor material on Pat Garrett and Oliver Lee.

Beach, Miss Mary D. — *Binghamton* [NY] Press, 6/30/1941: a highly personalized remembrance by an Apalachin friend and in-law; calls Rhodes a "modern Don Quixote."

Bloom, Lansing L. — *New Mexico Historical Review.* April, 1935, pp. 150/1: a personality sketch with photograph of Rhodes; reprints his poem, "A Blossom of Barren Lands."

—— *Dictionary of American Biography,* vol. XXI, pp. 625/6: a very personal appraisal of Rhodes as a man and as a writer. Most valuable.

Campbell, Alec [psuedonym] — *Zane Grey's Western Magazine,* July, 1950: "A New Start for the F C" being a short story based too closely upon chapters IV and V in BEYOND THE DESERT and so acknowledged by the author to the editor involved, Don Ward.

— *Zane Grey's Western Magazine,* Oct. 1951 and May, 1952: "No Sale" and "Bounty Man" being short stories whose lead character, "Stubby Parks," is based upon Rhodes and the stories upon happenings in his life.

Charles, Mrs. Tom — *New Mexico Magazine,* Feb., 1953: "Recollections of 'Gene Rhodes" being variations of anecdotes from Mrs. Rhodes biography and other sources.

—— *Tales of the Tularosa,* Alamogordo, 1953; rev. ed. 1954, pp. 1-13: expansion of the above article with inclusions from Rhodes' *Touring Topics* essays and Dobie's "My Salute to 'Gene Rhodes." Also, some sadly twisted facts about Rhodes by the woman who has done more than any other to keep his memory green in the third and last parish of his New Mexico province.

Designed and printed by Carl Hertzog, edited by Francis Fugate, this contains a magnificent Frontispiece of Rhodes by José Cisneros. The revised edition has a footnote, p. 7, concerning the statute of limitations and Rhodes' absence from New Mexico by Judge E. L. Mechem, Las Cruces, N. M.

—— *New Mexico Sun Trails,* Sept.Oct., 1955: "Memories of 'Gene Rhodes" is just about the same stuff as cited above, but rewritten.

Cleaveland, Mrs. Agnes Morley — *No Life for a Lady,* Boston, H M Co., 1941, pp. 278/287: sheds interesting light on Rhodes' early efforts to start a writing career.

Dunne, Brian Boru — If this columnist on the *Santa Fé New Mexican* ever gets his book finished, to be called *They All Come to Santa Fé* if he has his way, it will contain a chapter on Rhodes and his sojourn in Santa Fé during 1926/1927.

Fort, Lewis — *New Mexico Magazine,* Feb., 1944, "Poet on Horseback;" Oct., 1947, "Frontier Adventure;" March, 1948, "Tularosa Memory:" a series of articles dealing with Fort's stay at Rhodes' ranch in the San Andrés, 1900/1902. The first of these listed above was reprinted in *This is New Mexico,* edited by George Fitzpatrick, Santa Fé, 1948, pp. 69/75.

Fort's pieces are bathed in the warm nostalgia he felt for his youthful days when Rhodes had made a vivid and enduring impression upon him. They remained friends until Rhodes' death — and after.

Ferol, Raymond Egan — "The Place of the Cowboy Novel in American Literature," an unpublished Master's thesis, College of the Pacific, Stockton, Calif., June, 1950: contains superficial information about Rhodes' college days and his life in general.

Gordon, Dudley — *Los Angeles Westerners,* Keepsake 43, April, 1958: contains facsimile letter, Rhodes to C. F. Lummis, with set letter, Lummis to Rhodes, plus photographs both men, a poem by Lummis and brief editorial comment.

Gould, Charles N. — *Covered Wagon Geologist,* Norman, University Oklahoma Press, 1959; pp. VIII-IX, 233.

Gould was one of those great-hearted and overlooked men who roamed and knew the face of the West and did their damndest to save some part of it for the next generations. He and Rhodes were kindred spirits and enduring friends by letter, although they never met. In this long overdue autobiography, Gould died a decade past, he quotes "Sandy McGregor" and B. W. Beebe, in his Introduction, notes the kinship between Gould and Rhodes and has it pegged just right.

Haley, J. Evetts — *Jeff Milton, A Good Man With a Gun;* Norman, 1948, pp.

102/146: three chapters covering Milton's life in Socorro County and contiguous territory.

Milton gathered Kim Ki Roger's cattle when Rogers sold out to the Bar Cross syndicate. Haley's account of this and his recital of Rogers' rise to affluence closely parallels Rhodes' earlier writings, in both the "Old Timers" manuscript and THE TRUSTY KNAVES. Haley's footnotes indicate he got his information from other sources, Montagu Stevens, George Cook, Rube Pankey, Cole Railston, Jim Reed, all of whom were known intimately by Rhodes in his youth.

Rhodes was a boy of fifteen when Jeff Milton hit the Rio Grande valley. There is no doubt that Milton, a *Beau Sabreur* if ever there was one, made an indelible impression on Rhodes, not alone in mannerisms but in character and personal code. To read Haley's characterization of Milton and then compare Rhodes' fictional heroes with him is to prove the point.

The only probable direct appearance of Milton in Rhodes' fiction is as a minor character, *Tinnin*, in a short story written with Henry Wallace Phillips, "The Punishment and the Crime." That Rhodes did not use Jeff Milton, thinly disguised or under his own name, as he used so many others he had known is due, probably, to the fact that Rhodes, like Eugene Cunningham and others, knew that Jeff Milton was exceedingly "techy" about the use of his name in print.

Hoover, Edwin Hunt — *Author & Journalist*, Dec., 1927, "Eugene Manlove Rhodes Works Twenty Years on a Novel:" article based upon an interview over several days with Rhodes in 1927. Sheds interesting light upon the work habits of Rhodes by a man who had ridden the *Jornada del Muerto* with men of Rhodes' vintage and was a better than average writer about the West in his own right.

—— *Empire*, [Denver Post] 8/24/1952, pp. 14/15, "The Nameless Alemaños:" brief article on the origin of Aleman, New Mexico and how Rhodes found the grave cairn of that first nameless German.

Howard, Tom — *New Mexico Highway Journal*, April, 1929, "Gene Rhodes Remembers:" rambling, chatty interview with Rhodes while he was living at Three Rivers, N. M.

Hunt, Frazier — *Cap Mossman*, Hastings House, 1951: contains several anecdotes about Rhodes and Burton Mossman during the 1890s.

Hutchinson, W. H. — *Southwest Review*, Spring, 1956, "Grassfire on the Great Plains:" a rewrite of material on the Stuart Henry imbroglio gathered for the chapter on same in A BAR CROSS MAN.

—— *Empire*, [Denver Post] 4/22/1956, "The Incident Near Rincon": condensation of material unused in A BAR CROSS MAN.

—— *New Mexico Magazine*, April, 1956, "Cyrano in Chaps" and May, 1956, "Legends of a Lively Life": both rewritten condensations of material appearing in A BAR CROSS MAN.

Hynes, Frank J. — *Colophon, New Graphic Series*, Vol. I, No. 4, "A Memorandum for Rhodes Scholars": an account of how Rhodes annotated a copy of GOOD MEN AND TRUE for Robert Wilson Neal [cf Magazine List, 7/26/1913] This annotated copy is now owned by Vincent Starrett.

Jones, F. A. — *New Mexico Mines and Minerals*, Santa Fé 1905, Chapters XI, XII, XV: these specific chapters deal directly with locales intimately connected with Rhodes' life in New Mexico. The entire book is most valuable for a picture of the mining game in New Mexico as Rhodes knew it when a boy, youth, man.

Jones, Dr. Joseph — Bookplate designed by this faculty member of the University of Texas for the "Eugene Manlove Rhodes Memorial Book Shelf" he brought into being in 1956 in the Public Library at Tecumseh, Nebraska as part of that community's Centennial.

Keleher, Wm. A. — *The Fabulous Frontier*, The Rydal Press, Santa Fe, 1945; second printing, 1946; pp. 137/149 are devoted to Rhodes:

Minor errors of fact and mixed chronology cannot alter the "source" status of this book nor mitigate its importance to any understanding of the people, politics and scenes of Rhodes' early years. It is invaluable.

King, Frank M. — *Wranglin' the Past*, Los Angeles, 1935, Pasadena, 1946; Chapter XVI; *Pioneer Western Empire Builders*, Pasadena, 1946, Chapter 43: reminiscences about Rhodes by a genuine old-timer who had seen it through the smoke and was more garrulous than most of his contemporaries. Not important but interesting.

Knibbs, Henry H. — *The Riding Kid from Powder River*, Boston, 1919: this novel by a protogée depicts Rhodes' early years through the story character, "The Spider." Rhodes felt that the first 100 pages were accurate enough; thereafter, "His Knibbs" departed into the realm of fiction.

Kunitz & Haycraft — *Twentieth Century Authors*, New York, 1942, p. 1163: brief but accurate biographical sketch with photograph. It is interesting to note that Rhodes did not appear in *Living Authors*, by Dilly Tante, [*Stanley J. Kunitz*] New York, 1931, or subsequent printings of that edition.

McKenna, James A. — *Black Range Tales*, New York, 1936: nothing specific about Rhodes but most germane to the settings and characters of many of his stories, particularly STEPSONS OF LIGHT and THE PROUD SHERIFF.

Miller, Margaret — San Diego *Union*, 6/24/1934: brief, human-interest sketch by the wife of Max Miller, San Diego author and journalist.

Miller, Max — San Diego *Union*, 11/27/1949: review of THE BEST NOVELS, *etc* which is more a personal recall of Rhodes and his last years in Pacific Beach, Calif.

O'Neil, James B. — *They Die But Once*, Knight, New York, 1935: the most interesting of all association items.

O'Neil was the man who spearheaded the effort to print a uniform edition [*Bar Cross Edition*] of Rhodes' works in 1932/1933. This, actually, was a part of O'Neil's rehabilitation program, arranged by his friends, after he had done time in the Federal guest-house at McNeil's Island. Since his only crime was robbing a bank, this was no bar to Rhodes' befriending him.

Rhodes prodded O'Neil into taking-down for publication the reminiscences of Jeff Ake. References to Rhodes and quotations from his writings were larded into the book with a heavy hand by O'Neil and there are numerous anecdotes about Rhodes therein by Jeff Ake.

Ake had been foreman for John Riley in the 1890s, when Riley and

75

Rhodes hated one another most vigorously. Ake's son-in-law, Bob Burch, was wagon boss for Riley-Rynerson-Catron [the Tularosa Ranch] when these stalwarts of the Santa Fé Ring were jobbing Colonel Hinman Rhodes, 'Gene's father, out of his job as Agent for the Mescalero Apache, and trying to kill 'Gene in the process. That Rhodes took an interest in preserving Jeff Ake's reminiscences, that he liked him personally in these later years, is evidence as to the mellowing effect of time. The same ripe aging is again evidenced in Rhodes' treatment of Pat Garrett whom he once hated like the Devil hates a Baptist preacher.

Jeff Ake has been called "an authentic liar" by a man who should know. *Quien Sabe?* One thing is certain — this book has a flavor all its own.

Orcutt, Eddy — *Satevepost*, 8/20/1938, "Passed by Here, A Memorial to 'Gene Rhodes": warm-hearted appreciation of Rhodes, The Man, by a man who, himself, had a passionate heart.

Stuart N. Lake, he of *Wyatt Earp*, induced the *Post* to commission this article. Orcutt wanted to make it a two-part piece but Wesley Stout, then *Post* editor, dinged the double shot. After this piece appeared, Stout admitted to Orcutt that he had been wrong in his judgments. The response to this piece was such that a two-part story would have been more than justified.

Owego [NY] *Gazette* — Undated clipping, Rhodes' scrapbook, with same photo as used in WADDIES for Frontispiece; for a country paper, this was exceedingly long and covered Rhodes as a baseball player and enthusiast during his first sojourn in Apalachin, New York, 1906/1921.

Pearce, Thomas M. — *New Mexico Magazine*, June, 1940, "Literary Pilgrimage": this was the Coronado Quarto Centennial Edition of this magazine. Rhodes' grave, his burial and the like are described together with similar information on Mary Austin, A. F. Bandelier, C. F. Lummis, Emerson Hough and D. H. Lawrence.

Raine, Wm. MacLeod — *Author & Journalist*, Nov., 1922, "Western Fiction Discussed by Eugene Manlove Rhodes": more a study of Rhodes' work habits than the title indicates. It has been reprinted in *The Student Writer*, [np,nd] and in THE HIRED MAN ON HORSEBACK.
——— *The Brand Book*, 1945, Denver Westerners, Denver, 1946, pp. 47/58, "Eugene Manlove Rhodes, American": long, personal sketch of Rhodes written from the heart without diminution by factual details.
——— *Hoofs and Horns*, [Tuscon, Ariz.] March, 1947: a supposed review of WADDIES that became an appreciation of Rhodes, the man.
——— *Empire*, Denver Post Feb., 1948, " 'Gene Rhodes As I Knew Him": the major portion of a personality sketch of Rhodes that Raine had submitted to *Reader's Digest* without success. [It is worth noting that Eugene Cunningham tried to get an article about Rhodes in *Reader's Digest* about this same time, again without success. *See* item under May D. Rhodes hereafter]

Rhodes, May D. — *New Mexico Magazine*, June, 1939, June, July, August, 1940, June, 1941, August, 1942, Jan., 1943, Dec., 1944, March, 1945, May, 1947: this series of articles had a general title, "Fragments from a Frontier Memory," with individual sub-titles.

The material in these pieces is taken, virtually in entirety, from material that had appeared in her biography, THE HIRED MAN ON HORSEBACK. The piece for Jan., 1943, carries the joint byline of Jack D. Rhodes.

—— *Reader's Digest*, Jan., 1954, "My Most Unforgettable Character": a rewrite by Beth F. [*Mrs. Donald*] Day of previously published material.

Ristvedt, Mrs. Helen Smith — "Eugene Manlove Rhodes as Social Historian and Literary Artist," unpublished Master's thesis, Drake University, August, 1937: contains some personal material derived from correpondence with Eugene Cunningham, Mrs. Alexina Fall Chase and Mrs. Rhodes.

Shirley, Glenn — *Six-Gun and Silver Star*, Albuquerque, 1955, pp. 194/5, 198: discusses Bill Doolin's stay with Rhodes at the latter's ranch in the San Andrés.

Shirley makes the year 1895 while Rhodes, in letters to various friends, made it 1896. The essential fact of the visitation is not in dispute, which makes the disparity in times rather academic to this writer.

Sutherland, Wm. A. — *Out Where the West Be-Grins*, Southwest Publ. Co., Las Cruces [*NM*] 1942, pp. 11 & 27: two anecdotes about Rhodes by a man who was raised in the country and who's father was a close friend of Colonel Hinman Rhodes.

Thorp, N. Howard — *Literary Digest*, Aug. 21, 1920, "What's Become of the Punchers?": poem with three stanzas built around Rhodes in which he is mentioned by name.

—— *Pardner of the Wind*, [as told to Neil M. Clark] Caxton Printers, 1945 pp. 14 & 33: Clark compares Thorp to Rhodes as a writer; Thorp attributes a poem, "The Camp-Fire Has Gone Out," to Rhodes.

The whole book is studded with sidelights on places, people and events that were a part of Rhodes' early years. Thorp ranched alongside Rhodes in the San Andrés and there may have been a tenuous blood tie between the two through the Underwood family. Keleher's *The Fabulous Frontier* has some good material on Thorp.

Stratton, David H. — "Albert B. Fall and the Teapot Dome Affair," unpublished Doctoral, University of Colorado, 1955: notes Rhodes' friendship with Fall, quotes from several letters, Rhodes to Fall; nothing of importance.

Tilghman, Zoe A. — *Marshal of the Last Frontier*, Arthur H. Clark Co., Glendale [*Calif*] 1949, p. 229: mentions Bill Doolin staying with Rhodes.

Tully, Jim — *Biddy Brogan's Boy*, New York, 1942, pp. 265/7, 271, 276/7, 279: the character *Simon Lalend* in this autobiographical novel is Rhodes.

Tully gives credit to Rhodes for his help in launching Tully's writing career and pays tribute to Rhodes' human kindliness. This matter is discussed more fully in A BAR CROSS MAN.

Yore, Clem — *Hoofs and Horns*, Feb., 1935: untitled, memorial article on Rhodes by a man who was a prolific and more than competent writer of "westerns."

It is possible to close this section with a most interesting and revealing association item through the courtesy of Mr. Harrison Leussler.

This is a copy of Captain William French's *Some Recollections of a Western Ranchman*, [Stokes, NY, n. d.] which Rhodes annotated for Leussler and in which he wrote a long inscription about the book. French, a cultured, hot-blooded young

Irishman, arrived in New Mexico shortly before Christmas, 1883 and went ranching near Alma, under the Mogollons, with the W S iron. The region and the times are covered, also, by James H. Cook's *Fifty Years on the Frontier* of which Rhodes said: "Not so fine a book as this."

Rhodes' inscription is followed by his notations from the book:

"Dear Leussler:

"I despair of any means of letting you know how fine this book seems to me. You see, I know the men, places and events. In the nature of things, most of my notes are to show some degree of modification or dissent. That means, neglecting fractions, that where I make no notes, I am thoroughly satisfied.

"Now turn to page 2 — 'Upcher, Hardcastle and Lyon, recent graduates of Cambridge.' Here is one story French does not tell. Lyon and Campbell, Upcher, Hardcastle, Wilson, Montagu Stevens and French were (socially) birds of a feather. They arranged to get together for a good old English dinner . . . don't you know? Unfortunately, some of them were ardent Catholics — and some were ardently otherwise. Wine. And when there was less wine than when the dinner began — these young men fought again the Battle of the Boyne.

"The lot were pretty well banged up. Country of enormous distances and some of the cripples had hard work getting home.

"Tempus fidgetted — as tempus does. The wiser and older heads got together and — a year later — arranged for a reconciliation and another dinner to celebrate their maturity and wisdom. Wine again — and the Third Battle of the Boyne.

"When we compare this book with other 'memoirs' we see that it was written by a gentleman. I know of no volume which shows so little egotism. I had some thought of reviewing the book. I could not do it without putting more 'ego' into the review than Captain French did in the book.

Yours,
Eugene M. Rhodes."

Page 2 — this note: "Scott was foreman of the Bar W, 40,000 head of cattle. He had family, brains, education and opportunity. He killed himself in Tularosa. 'Why did ye also give to me / Beauty and truth to know / The ears to hear and the eyes to see / And the hands that let all go?' "

Pages 26/27 — French was in the hotel at Socorro when Joel Fowler knifed a man who refused to drink with him. French dubs him " . . . an unfortunate stranger in the clothing line who had gone to the bar-room for a cigar."

Rhodes noted this as follows: "Curious mistake. The man killed was Jim Yale — saloon keeper at Engle. The day before he was killed I tried to sell Jim a six shooter. Jim said he had no use for it — that he never had any trouble. And Elfego Baca in his book gives still another name for the murdered man. If it wasn't Jim who was killed, that is a joke on Jim for we buried him." [See *Desperadoes of New Mexico*, Father Stanley, Denver, 1935, p. 267, for yet another name of Fowler's last victim which is closer to Rhodes' choice than Baca's.]

Pages 46/47 — On Elfego Baca's fight at Milligan's [*Middle*] Plaza:

"Clem Hightower was in this disorder. In fact, it was Clem, with Jerome Martin, who stopped it. Liquor was the trouble."

Page 52 — On the manner of Elfego's going-in with the deputy sheriff:

"The Parade was as follows. Elfego kept his two guns and rode in the back seat of the buckboard with a gun in the small of the deputy's back. He notified the ten or twelve cowboys who proposed to lynch him that they were to stay in front of the buckboard — that if one of them dropped back, he [Elfego] would kill the deputy. They stayed in front."

Page 214 — where the old drifter is riding a bad horse and the saddle turns with him — "This is fine stuff — and true to life."

Page 226 — apparently a general comment on the book as a whole:

"This is as authentic a story of the cow country as I have ever known. There people told you the truth — to your face. *They* didn't *have to lie*. Very fine yarn. Seems like a letter from home."

Page 228 — where French discusses the range war between the Hall family and the L C outfit:

"Tom Hall was killed near Engle about 1911 in a fight with five outlaws. He was a fine man." [See WHH's mention of this under "Consider the Lizard" in THE BEST NOVELS ETC.]

Page 229 — where French mentions Cole Railston as being foreman of Hampson's Double Circles:

"Foreman of the Bar Cross and the V Cross T. I worked for him 13 years. Still living. He appears in many of my stories." [He was Cole *Ralston* in the stories. Not for a typically thin Rhodesian disguise but simply because Rhodes did not learn the correct spelling of his name until he returned to New Mexico in 1926.]

Page 251 — which starts Chapter XVII, headed THE WILD BUNCH:

"This episode of the Wild Bunch working for the W S *is the joke* of all time."

Pages 258/259 — Where French says "I was frequently congratulated by the merchants of Magdalena on having such a well behaved outfit";

"Just so. I had outlaws working on my ranch for years. But they were on their good behavior there. Elsewhere was too hot for them — and they didn't want to attract attention."

Page 262 — where French discusses the robbery of the Colorado & Southern passenger train near Folsom, New Mexico:

"I was urged to go with these boys on this train robbery — but I was flush."

Pages 264/265 — where French speaks slightingly of Sam Ketchum:

"This is really too bad. Sam was an old man — past 60. Bullet travelled all the way up his left arm as he was firing a rifle. Shattered bone in four places — and he died from the wound. Sam had been working for me six months. Rode directly from my place to Folsom."

Pages 272/273 — where French tells of Charles Siringo's visit to him and the photograph of the Wild Bunch Siringo had wherein French identified his foreman, Jim Lowe, and learns that he is really Butch Cassidy of whom French says: ". . . he was the best trail boss I had ever seen and one of the best men the W S had in their employ since I had known them."

"This is true — and Butch Cassidy refused *to kill,* under great provocation — or necessity."

Page 283 — where French speaks of his distaste for Socorro:

"The most corrupt town in the United States."

IN THE DUST OF THE DRAG

[No derogation of the authors or material listed in this section
is intended by such inclusion.]

Adventure — "Camp Fire" section, 11/20/1924, pp. 177/181: prints letters in
the Henry/Hough controversy, mentions Rhodes as the instigator thereof
and contains a tribute to the validity, freshness and readability of Rhodes'
writings by *W.F.G.* [unidentified]

—— "Camp Fire" section, 12/30/1924, pp. 175/6: a letter from Rhodes on
the West and its code.

Agnew, Seth M. — *Saturday Review*, 3/14/1953, "God's Country and the
Publisher": essay on the sustained commercial endurance of the "western."
Mentions Rhodes in the list of stalwarts such as Raine, Luke Short, Wm.
Colt MacDonald and Alan LeMay who have turned out "action, color and
interest."

Atkinson, Will — *Land of Freedom*, [n.p.] April, 1927, published by Capon
Springs Water Company, Capon Springs, West Virginia: contains quotations
from COPPER STREAK TRAIL and lists Rhodes' books to-date with comments by Atkinson who was a Rhodesian from who laid the chunk.

Benét, Wm. Rose — *The Reader's Encyclopedia*, New York, 1948, p. 923: lists
Rhodes' principal books and says "He was a cowboy for 25 years and knew
thoroughly the life of which he wrote."

—— *Saturday Review of Literature*, 9/2/1933, in "The Phoenix Nest:"
quotes letter from Rhodes; 1/20/1934, same department; prints letter from
Rhodes and a nonsense poem, "Tuhid Asone."

Botkin, B. A. — *A Treasury of Western Folklore*, New York, 1951, p. 326:
cites THE TRUSTY KNAVES as the first explanation of Bill Doolin's
hideout after he broke jail in Guthrie, Oklahoma.

Burke, W. J. and Howe, Will D. — *American Authors and Books - 1640/1940*,
New York, 1943, pp. 626/7: lists Rhodes' novels, gives dates of birth and
death.

Brayton, Howard — *New Mexico Magazine*, Nov., 1949: mentions THE BEST
NOVELS, etc in the column, "Southwestern Bookshelf."

Broome, Bertram — *New Mexico Magazine*, Jan., 1939: letter about Rhodes
in section "The Mail Bag."

Calvin, Ross — *"Pasó Por Aquí"*, July 7, 1934: a paper read by Calvin before
the Second New Mexico Round Table on Southwest Literature, Las Vegas,
N. M.

Deep emotion under admirable control distinguishes this interpretation
of Rhodes' character and of his kinship with the land Calvin had come to
love as his own. [*See* Calvin's *Sky Determines* for evidence of this love]

Charles, Mrs. Tom — *El Paso* [Texas] *Times, Alamogordo* [NM] *News*, various issues, 1946/1958: Mrs. Charles, who lives in Alamogordo, also acts as
correspondent for the El Paso paper upon any Rhodesian occasion. These
items mainly concern establishment of the annual pilgrimage to Rhodes'
grave and related matters whereby Rhodes' name could be kept alive and

80

Alamogordo could benefit thereby. The first pilgrimage was held in 1953 and annually thereafter.

Coan & Lillard — *America in Fiction*, Stanford University Press, Stanford, Calif., 3rd. ed., 1949: cites GOOD MEN AND TRUE under "Grass," p. 11, as "debunking some of the cowboy legend;" cites COPPER STREAK TRAIL under "Mountain and Desert," p. 18, for "gunplay and cowboy humor."

Coleman, Rufus A. — *Western Prose and Poetry*, New York & London, 1932, p. 487: mentions only.

Colum, Padraic — *New Mexico Quarterly*, Spring, 1949: writing in appreciation of Alice Corbin Henderson, Colum mentions her friendship with Rhodes.

Dale, Edward Everett — Cow Country, Norman [Okla.] 1942, p. 254: mentions.

[Unknown] — *Dictionary North American Authors*, Ryerson Press, Toronto, Canada, 1951: cites Rhodes' appearances in various compendiums of biographical information.

Durling, E. V. — San Francisco *Examiner*, 7/25/1955: daily column on editorial page, mentions Rhodes as one writer of western stories who had real experience as a cowboy.

Associated Press — *El Paso* [Texas] *Herald*, 2/25/1928: prints AP story from Hillsboro, N. M., about sale of Jacob Dines Ranch by Cole Railston to Miguel Otero which mentions Rhodes and his novel, STEPSONS OF LIGHT.

Fergusson, Erna — *Our Southwest*, New York, 1941, pp. 26 & 368: makes mention of Rhodes.

—— *New Mexico*, New York, 1951, p. 403: lists THE BEST NOVELS, etc., among books for "Further Reading."

Frothingham, Robert — *Songs of Men*, Cambridge, 1918: acknowledges Rhodes' help in compiling the contents of the book.

—— *Songs of Horses*, Cambridge, 1920: in Foreword, uses verse about The Little Eohippus.

Gard, Wayne — *Sam Bass*, Boston, 1936, pp. 231/2: quotes letter from Rhodes to Will Williams, [Denton, Texas] about Frank Jackson, the *compadre* of Sam Bass.

Gilman, C. P. — *Saturday Review Literature*, 8/9/1924: letter asking why Rhodes is not better known. Quoted by J. Frank Dobie in his "My Salute to Gene Rhodes."

Hafen, LeRoy and Rister, Carl Coke — *Western Culture*, New York, 1950, 2nd. Ed., p. 661: mentions.

Haney, John L. — *Story of Our Literature*, New York, 1923, p. 365: lists Rhodes' books under "Supplemental Reading."

Harkness, David James — *The Southwest and West Coast in Literature*, University of Tennessee, Knoxville, 1954: mentions Rhodes under "New Mexico Fiction."

Hinkel, Edgar J. [Editor] — *Bibliography of California Fiction, Poetry and Drama*, WPA Project 6463, sponsored by The Alameda County Library,

Oakland, Calif., 1938, mimeographed: Vol. I, pp. 292/3, lists Rhodes novels and shows his residence as California from 1917/1934.
—— *Criticism of California Liturature*, [same project and sponsor as above] 1940, mimeographed; Vol. 3, pp. 750/53, gives abstracts of reviews of Rhodes' books as taken from *Book Review Digest*.

Horan, James D. and Gann, Paul — *Pictorial History of the Wild West*, New York, 1954, p. 170: mentions Bill Doolin being at Rhodes' ranch; apparently from Botkin without provenance.

Hot Springs [*NM*] *Herald* — 6/12/1953: an anecdote about Rhodes by Robert Martin.

Hunter, Bob and Britzman, Homer — *Arizona Highways*, Sept., 1952: article on J. R. Williams with several mentions of Rhodes who, with Charley Russell, is used by the authors to make a standard of comparison for Jim Williams' own cartoons.

Johnson, E. Dana — *Santa Fe New Mexico*, 3/7/1928: editorial on Governor R. C. Dillon's alleged pardon of Rhodes and Rhodes' contemplated book on New Mexico's Old-Timers; 3/7/1928: news story printing the pardon with brief comment by Rhodes on scope and nature of the book; 6/28/1934: editorial obituary "Good Man and True;" 6/29/1934: news story about Gene's body being taken to the San Andrés; 3/15-3/18-3/20/1935: series of columns about trip to Rhodes' grave by Johnson and members of the Rhodes Memorial Association; 5/19/1941: long news story, 3 full-page columns, about forthcoming graveside ceremonies and dedication with resumé of Rhodes' life.

Laughlin, Ruth — *Caballeros*, Caxton edition, Caldwell, 1945, p. 109: mentions and misspells name as *Rhoades*.

Las Cruces *Sun News* — 12/8/1946: minor biographical remarks about Rhodes.

[*Obituary Notices*] — Eddy Orcutt put Gene's death notice on the AP wire from San Diego: unless otherwise noted, this was used by the papers listed below.
El Paso Herald-Post, 6/28/1934, obituary and tribute to Rhodes' veracity by Betty Luther; *Los Angeles Examiner*, 6/28/1934, *Los Angeles Times*, 6/28/1934, with portrait and heading "Ex-Cowboy In Last Round-Up"; *New York Times*, 6/28/1934, with additional material on his life in New York state from their morgue; *Publisher's Weekly*, 7/7/1934, rewrite of Orcutt's material; *San Diego Tribune*, 6/27/1934 with follow-up, 6/30/1934; *San Diego Union* 6/28/1934 with follow-up, 6/29/1934.

Owego [*NY*] *Gazette* — 7/5/1934: account of memorial services held for Rhodes in Apalachin, 7/1/1934, with Eulogy by Rev. George D. Beach and Tribute by Alan H. Rhodes; prints poem "When I Come Into Mine Estate."

Hart, James D. — *Oxford Companion to American Literature*, New York, 1941, p. 635/6: biographical sketch, partial bibliography, etc.

Pattee, Fred L. — *New American Literature*, New York, 1930, p. 118: mentions.

Payne, Leonidas W. — *A Survey of Texas Literature*, New York, Chicago, San Francisco, 1928, p. 30: mentions.

Pearce, Thomas M. — *New Mexico Quarterly*, May, 1934: mentions in "Southwestern Roots," this issue.

Peyton, Green — *American's Heartland, The Southwest*, Norman, 1948, p. 226: mentions.

Raine, William Mac L. — *The Desert's Price*, Garden City, 1924; dedicated to Rhodes.

Raine, Wm. Mac L. and Barnes, Will C. — *Cattle*, Garden City, 1930, p. 83: mentions.

Raines, Lester [Editor] — *Writers and Writings of New Mexico*, Las Vegas, 1934, mimeographed: pp. 104/105 have a biographical sketch and reviews of several books by Esther B. Hazen; pp. 106/107 contain Ross Calvin's tribute to Rhodes aforementioned.

—— *More New Mexico Writers and Writings*, Las Vegas, 1935, mimeographed: p. 64 has reviews of BEYOND THE DESERT and THE PROUD SHERIFF.

—— *The Literature of New Mexico*, Las Vegas, 1936, mimeographed: p. 84 is reprint of biographical sketch from the first of this series.

Rhoades, Nelson Osgood — *The Rhodes Family in America*, Vol. I, No. 3, Los Angeles, February, 1920, p. 9: mentions Rhodes' descent and has paragraph on his stories of the West.

Riegel, Robert — *America Moves West*, New York, 1930, p. 541: mentions.

Robinson, Will — *Roswell [NM] Dispatch*, 12/3/1946: recall of early days with Rhodes by a fellow-partisan of Oliver Lee during the Fountain/Garrett trouble.

Tisdale, Mrs. E. E. — Master's thesis in process, 1958, Belgrade, Montana.

Santee, Ross — *Lost Pony Tracks*, New York, 1953, pp. 143/4: anecdotes from Earl Pierce [*"who saw much of Rhodes"*] about 'Gene's way with horses, his reading while riding, his never letting a bad horse spook him.

[It will be a long time, if ever, before a book comes close to touching this one for the sensory perceptions, the fidelities to life and its details, the emotional recalls of men and horses, that Ross Santee encompassed here. The *best* of all memoirs about the West-That-Was]

Sonnichsen, C. L. — *Cowboys and Cattle Kings*, Norman, 1950: cites Rhodes as one of the *puros* who wrote from the inside-out.

Tinker, Edward L. — *The Horsemen of the Americas and the Literatures They Have Inspired*, New York, 1953: a brief sketch of Rhodes based upon commonly accepted hearsay appears on pp. 110/111; a list of his books graces pp. 146/7.

[Rhodes was mentioned in the pamphlet issued by Princeton University for their exhibition of materials from this book]

Tressman, Ruth — *New Mexico Hist. Review*, Jan., 1951, "Home on the Range,": quotes Rhodes.

Tucker, Mary — *Books of the Southwest*, New York, 1939, pp. 93/4: mentions.

Vaden, Clay — *New Mexico Quarterly*, Feb., 1936: reviews *They Die But Once* and mentions Rhodes.

Interesting because of Vaden's position as editor of the *Catron County Herald*, Quemado, N. M.

White, Owen P. — *Autobiography of a Durable Sinner*, New York, 1942, p. 121: an anecdote about Rhodes of which it has been said by a man who knew them both *"Some Lies are worse than others!"*

[Unknown] — *Who's Who Among North American Authors*. Golden Syndicate Publ. Co., Los Angeles: Vol. IV, 1929/30, has biographical sketch with numerous errors plus list of periodicals in which Rhodes had published; Vol. V, 1931/32, corrects misspelling of Mrs. Rhodes' name; Vol. VI, 1933/35, shows death and adds books to bibliography.

[Unknown] — *Who's Who In America*: Rhodes appears in each issue from 1916/17 to and including 1936/37.

[Unknown] — *Who Was Who in America*, 1941: brief sketch, misdates death.

SOME CHARACTERS IN RHODES' STORIES

In many cases, Rhodes did not bother to change the real-life names of his people when he transferred them to his fiction. In many cases, too, he gave the real-life name story characteristics that had belonged to other real-life people. It has not been possible, nor actually desirable, to identify all the characters in the Rhodesian stories. Enough identification has been made to prove the truth of Eugene Cunningham's statement about Eugene Rhodes: *"He could not create people. He could only, and upon my marrowbones I thank Mr. Swinburne's Gods for it, photograph in color, record in faintest intonation, real people that he knew."* The following list has fictional name in italic, life derivation in regular type.

Armstrong, Polk — Polk Armstrong, [see *Andy Hinkle*]

Aughinbaugh, George — George T. Aughinbaugh, a young Easterner whom Rhodes met at the home of Lewis Fort, a young Louisianian, in Roswell, N.M., 1905.

Baca, Octaviano — Elfego Baca, he of *Law and Order, Ltd.*

Baird, Gene — Eugene Baird, son of "Uncle Jim" Baird who ranched in the White Sands below Organ Gap.

Ballinger, Leo — Reo Barringer, transplanted Easterner.

Barela, Anastacio — Anastacio Barela, deputy-sheriff of Doña Ana county, etc.

Beebe, Billy — William B. Barbee, a Texian, rider for the John Cross; "an indomnitable will, a violent temper and a prodigious memory." An authority on the Punic Wars, he could quote Shakespeare "like Leviticus quoting the Good Book itself." The name Beebe came from a neighbor of Rhodes in Apalachin, N.Y.

Bird, Charley — William "Cherokee Bill" Kellum, friend and partisan of Oliver Lee who left his nickname on a canyon in Lincoln National Forest.

Bojorquez, Frank — Francisco Bojórquez, wagon boss for the John Cross, *Baja California* born, the best bronc rider and roper in the country, with common

84

sense to amount to genius. Later sheriff of Sierra County and member of the state legislature. Will Rogers saw him rope at Calgary when Bojórquez was past sixty, never wasting a loop, with a patriarchal beard that endeared him to the crowd. He and Felipe Lucero explain why the Hispanic New Mexicans in Rhodes' stories are human beings.

Bransford, Jeff — Jefferson Davis Bransford, discussed under BRANSFORD IN ARCADIA.

Carpenter, Jack — Warren Carpenter, first wagon boss for the Bar Cross, killed by lightning on the *Jornada.*

Cafferty, Ben — Ben Williams, as discussed under THE LITTLE WORLD WADDIES.

Chandler, Tip — Jack Chandler, discussed under THE PROUD SHERIFF.

Collins, Jimmy — Gene Rhodes, as a boy.

The Colonel — Sometimes Phillips Mothersill, manager of the Bar Cross, sometimes Willard Hopewell, of the John Cross. Both men appear, also, under their own names.

Copeland, Bud — Gene Rhodes, in his twenties.

Creagan, Ben — Ben Williams again.

Cremony, Bat — John Dolan, of the Lincoln County War, an associate of John H. Riley, *et al,* then and later.

Dines, Johnny — John Dines, discussed under STEPSONS OF LIGHT.

Espalin, José — José Espalin, deputy-sheriff under Garrett.

Foster, George — George Foster, Texian, rider for Bar Cross and 7 T X. Had first well-drilling rig on the *Jornada* in 1902. [See McCall, William.]

Fowler, Jake — John H. Riley, of the Lincoln County War and the Santa Fé Ring. The name *Fowler* was derived from Joel Fowler, lynched at Socorro [NM] in 1884 for one killing too many.

Foy, Christopher — Oliver Milton Lee who deserves a book, not a note or even such discussion as is found under THE DESIRE OF THE MOTH.

Frenger, Numa — Numa Frenger as discussed under PASÓ POR AQUÍ.

Fuentes, Helen Mar — Miss Helen Mar MacGregor gave two names to this fictional heroine.

Gandy, Joe — Ben Williams for the third time; discussed more fully under LITTLE WORLD WADDIES.

Garrett, Pat — Patrick Floyd Garrett, discussed under THE DESIRE OF THE MOTH and PASÓ POR AQUÍ. He makes another, and an unfavorable, appearance in an early short story, "Wildcat Represents," as *The Tall Sycamore.*

Gifford, Bobby — Alfred Heinemann, a Los Angeles youth who stayed some months with Rhodes in the San Andrés.

Graham, Charlie — Charles J. Graham, who leased and later bought Rhodes' homestead. He married a half-sister of Oliver Lee and rode for the Bar Cross under both Railston and McCombs who dubbed him "A fine hand and a fine citizen."

Hall, Tom — Tom Hall, Texian, member of a family who fought the LC outfit for the waters of Mule Spring in the Mogollons. A partisan of Oliver Lee during the trouble over Colonel Fountain's disappearance.

Hamilton, Bill and Hamilton, Buck — Kinney Hamilton, deputy-sheriff of Otero county. Killed by Claude Barbee at Rhodes' ranch.

85

Harkey, Pete and Harkey, Edith — Dee Harkey, discussed under STEPSONS OF LIGHT, with the girl based upon Miss May Bailey of Las Cruces.

Hines, "Pretty" Pierre — Pierre R. Hines, a student at New Mexico College of Mines, Socorro, who loaned books to Rhodes. Now a mining engineer of Portland, Oregon.

Hinkle, Andy — Polk Armstrong, discussed under THE PROUD SHERIFF, who appears, also, under his own name in other stories.

Hopewell, Colonel — Willard S. Hopewell, born in Chester, England; a blockade-runner during the Civil War and a professional revolutionist in South America before coming to Sierra County, N.M., about 1879. He promoted, organized and managed the John Cross outfit [*J-Half Circle-Cross*] also called "The California Company." In Rhodes' words, "A most interesting man."

Hughes, Caradoc — Caradoc Hughes, a Welsh miner; "He can break more rock than any man who walks." Killed for camp-robbing while working for Rhodes' brother, Clarence, in Old Mexico.

James, Emil — Emil James, twice Sheriff of Socorro County.

Jastrow — H. A. Jastro, president of The Victorio Land & Cattle Co., Deming, N.M., who bought cattle, too, for Miller & Lux, the great California operators.

Jim-Ike-Bob — James B. Gililland, son of a Quantrell raider, staunch friend and associate of Oliver Lee. "A happy man. His laugh would blow off your hat."

Slick Johnny — John H. Riley, more directly from Rhodes' opinions of him.

Johnson, Pete — Pete Johnson, foreman of the Bar W out of Carizozo, N.M.

Jones, Neighbor — Neighbor Jones, discussed under HIT THE LINE HARD: a surveyor by trade who taught Rhodes cribbage and pinochle.

Lewis, Bob — Robert Lewis, chronic deputy-sheriff in Socorro County.

Lewis, Pres — Preston G. Lewis, from tidewater Virginia. Miner, blacksmith, freighter, close friend of Col. Rhodes; "Pres Lewis was my earliest hero, he looked like Jove. He was 45 when I was 13." See under THE TRUSTY KNAVES.

Lindauer, Herman — Sygmund Lindauer, discussed under THE TRUSTY KNAVES.

Lipton, Tobe — Tobe Tipton, saloon and hotel-keeper of Tularosa.

Llewellyn, Clint — Clinton Llewellyn, deputy-sheriff under Garrett, son of W.H.H.Llewellyn, prominent "Santa Fé Ring" Republican.

Lucero, Felipe — Felipe Lucero, member of a prominent clan, rider for the Bar Cross, descendant of a man who rode with Peñalosa. Sheriff of Doña Ana County at the time Pat Garrett was killed.

Marble, John — John Meadows, rancher, long-time friend of Rhodes.

Martin, The Honorable Robert; also, Bob Martin. — Robert Martin, came to the *Jornada* in 1892, a boy of 19, from four years as a rider for the Bell Ranch in Texas. Foreman of the 7 T X two years later; lifelong resident of that country with a distinguished record of public service.

McCall, Bill — William McCall, a Bar Cross rider. He, George Foster and Henry Summerford all homesteaded on the Rio Grande, around Salem and Garfield, and are depicted thusly in THE LITTLE WORLD WADDIES.

McComas, Dallas — Carroll W. McCombs, a Texian who came to the Bar Cross in 1886/7 and rode for them until 1898, barring the summer of 1890 when he went beyond the Yellowstone with a Double Circle trail herd from Texas.

Took over the Bar Cross wagon when Cole Railston quit in 1896 and ran it until he delivered the Bar Cross cattle to Levi Baldwin in 1898.

McEwen, Ross — Ross McMillan, discussed under PASÓ POR AQUÍ.

McNew, Bill — W. H. McNew, married a niece of Oliver Lee. His ranch was, and is still, near Orogrande, N. M.

Morgan, Springtime — Springtime Morgan is the way the country knew him. A man of some letters, quite a musician, came from Kentucky with funds of his own. Staked Polk and Frank Armstrong to a saloon in San Marcial. Had a ranch in the San Mateo Mountains, prospected, lived alone.

Mossman, Burt — Burton C. Mossman, of Arizona Ranger fame. Mossman, two years older than Rhodes, came to New Mexico when his family settled below Las Cruces after the Civil War. Rhodes met him first in 1887, when Mossman repped on the *Jornada* work for the Bar A Bar, becoming foreman of that outfit the next year, just after he turned 21. He and Rhodes were close friends so long as Mossman stayed in that country.

Murray, Pink — Pink Murray, wagon boss for the John Cross.

Panky, Bill — Tom Tucker with a version of Rube Pankey's patronym. Tucker was a Texian who went to Arizona with the Hashknife outfit and was one of the first casualties in the Tonto Basin War. Recovering, he went to work for Oliver Lee, siding him in the Lee/Good trouble, and during the Fountain case. He was an amazing and an unusual man, of whom Oliver M. Lee, Jr. wrote as follows: "Tucker was a big man with a chest about two feet wide. In later years I had occasion to sleep in the same room and never saw him do except the same every night — He would lie flat on his back with his pistol on his chest." Rhodes always intended to write Tom Tucker true to life and life-sized but never did.

Pardee, Johnny — Gene Rhodes and Johnny Dines.

Patterson, Erie — Kim Ki Rogers, discussed under THE TRUSTY KNAVES.

Peso — Peso, chief of police, Mescalero Agency, during Col. Rhodes tenure there.

Pierce, Sticky — Ed Pierce, V Cross T rider.

Priesser, Aloys — Aloys Priesser, discussed under THE PROUD SHERIFF.

Pringle, John Wesley — Discussed under GOOD MEN AND TRUE. Two of his names, and something of his character, came from John Wesley Green; Sergeant, 15th U. S. Infantry, against the Apache, 1880/1885; served in Troop G, Rough Riders, "The Big Four Regiment," and served as superintendent, Territorial Penitentiary.

Ralston, Cole — Cole Railston, wagon boss for the Bar Cross, 1890/1896, and rode for them before taking the wagon. Ranched successfully out of Magdalena, N. M., for many years before his death in 1949.

Rainboldt, Dick — Will Rainboldt, of Roswell, N. M.

River, Neuces — Pat Garrett again.

Rogers, Kim Ki — Kim Ki Rogers; under his own name in "The Line of Least Resistance." [*see Erie Patterson*] He started the K I M brand out of Engle about 1883, selling out to the Bar Cross about 1886.

Ross, Tom — T. J. Ross, wagon boss for the John Cross; started his own *Ladder* brand in the early 1890s.

Scarboro, George — George Scarborough, discussed under STEPSONS OF LIGHT.

See, Charlie — 'Gene Rhodes for the most part.

Simpson, Bill — William Simpson, a John Cross rider.

Summerford, Henry — Henry Summerford, a Bar Cross man; [*see Bill McCall*]

Sutherland, Dave — D. M. Sutherland, pioneer merchant and postmaster of La Luz, N. M.

Tegardner, Uncle Ben — Ben Teagarden or Teagarten; a man in his seventies when Rhodes first came to Engle, N. M., who had seen the elephant all over the world. A pioneer of the *Jornada del Muerto*, a true frontiersman of the early Far West, he left an indelible impression upon 'Gene Rhodes.

Thompson, Steve "Wildcat" — Hiram Yoast in "The Come-On;" otherwise a Gene Rhodes/Yoast composite.

Thorgood or Thorogood — Eugene Thorogood, an educated Englishman who ranched on the sacaton flats east of Mockingbird Gap. He had a flair for books and reading and was quite a crony of Rhodes.

Weir, Jody — J. D. Weir, discussed under STEPSONS OF LIGHT.

White, Foamy — Gene Rhodes.

Yost, Hiram — Hiram Yoast, discussed under "The Come-On".

Rhodes populated many of his western settings with Easterners and wrote many short stories, chief among them "The Prince of Tonight," "A Ragtime Lady," "The God from the Machine," entirely devoted to Eastern life, scenes and people. While they are undoubtedly true to life, as Rhodes saw it there, they are not discussed here nor are the characters pursued beyond their fictional roles for the simple reason that it is not as a fictionist or archaeologist of the Atlantic seaboard that Gene Rhodes will be remembered.

In his short story, "The Ragged Twenty-Eighth," Rhodes faithfully portrayed his father, Colonel Hinman Rhodes, and his father's regiment, 28th Illinois Volunteer Infantry, as they made a part of U. S. Grant's successful sundering of the Confederacy. In "The Brave Adventure" Rhodes gave a good factual account, heavily charged with his father's personal emotions, of the Battle of Shiloh. In this story, too, he gave a good honest reportage of pioneer life in Schuyler County, Illinois during the 1840s when his mother's people, the Manloves, first settled there.

REAL AND FICTIONAL COMMUNITIES IN RHODES' STORIES

In many stories, Rhodes used the real name of the community he depicted from life, Hillsboro, Garfield, El Paso, etc. In others, he disguised the town's name without changing its characteristics. It has been possible to relate the fictional to the real names for most of Rhodes important places.

Fictional Name	Real Name
Abingdon	Apalachin, New York.
Arcadia	Alamogordo, New Mexico.
Argentine	Silver City, N. M.
Dundee	Engle, N. M.
Heart's Desire	White Oaks, N. M.
Las Uvas	Las Cruces, N. M.
La Huerta	La Luz, N. M.
Mecca	Alamogordo, N. M.
Oasis	Tularosa, N. M.
Rainbow's End	La Luz, N. M.
Ridgepole	Magdalena, N. M.
Salamanca	Carrizozo, N. M.
San Clemente	Composite of the Black Range mining towns of Kingston, Chloride, Fairview and Grafton, N. M.
San Lucas	Las Cruces, N. M.
Saragossa	Socorro, N. M.
Shard	Alma, N. M.
Target	Deming, N. M.
Temporal	Tularosa, N. M.
Tripoli	Doña Ana, N. M.
Vesper	Owego, New York.

COW OUTFITS IN RHODES' LIFE AND FICTION

Anchor X — Ranged on the east side of the Rio Grande, at the head of Monticello Canyon almost on the plains of San Augustin. The old *Ojo Caliente* Army post was their headquarters. The cattle were sold to Levi Baldwin in 1899, $10.00 a head with calves throwed in, and the ranches were acquired by Solomon Luna.

Bar A Bar — Owned by Langford & Carpenter, of Colorado, they headquartered just east of the town of Monticello, ranging down that same canyon to the Rio Grande. They claimed some 8,000 head when Burton Mossman took over the wagon in 1888 but were drouthed out by 1893.

Bar Cross — Had its inception in 1886 when the Detroit & Rio Grande Live Stock Company, a Michigan syndicate headed by General Russell A. Alger, governor of Michigan and a prominent Republican politician, bought out Kim Ki Roger's K I M brand. Colonel Phillips Mothersill, from Detroit, came out to Engle to be general manager and remained in this capacity until 1898 when the cattle were sold to Levi Baldwin who shipped them out.

The Bar Cross held the black grama range of the *Jornada del Muerto* between the San Andrés and Caballo Mountains, from Engle, where the Armendariz Grant boundaries reached their farthest south, to Fort Selden, Rincon for todays' maps. Their maximum tally was some 14,000 head.

The brand originally was Bar N Cross, on the left neck, shoulder and side in that order. This was changed to Bar Cross, in 1891. They retained the K I M as a horse brand during the life of the outfit.

The headquarters were at Engle always although the wagon worked out of Aleman after 1890 when the Bar Cross acquired the gigantic house built there by John Martin after he dug the first well on the *Jornada* about 1867. This was the outfit for whom Rhodes worked more, and more continuously, than any other. They leased his homestead in the San Andrés as a horse camp and the Bar Cross always was the epitome to Rhodes of the Free Range days — "Our cooks would fry anything once."

The outfit had four wagon bosses during its career: Warren Carpenter, Frank Wallace, Cole Railston and Carroll McCombs. McCombs has furnished the monthly wage scale in effect while he was running the wagon which affords a comparison with today's values: Wagon Boss, $75.00; Ramrod, $35/40.00; top hands, $35.00; average hands, $30.00; bronc rider, $30/40.00; day wrangler, $25/30.00; night hawk, $30.00; cook, $30/-40.00; cook's swamper, $30.00.

Bar W — Known as The Carrizozo Company with headquarters eleven miles from White Oaks in Lincoln County. Originally owned by Major L. G. Murphy, of Lincoln County War notoriety, it was owned by Thomas B. Catron and his brother-in-law, E. A. Walz, in 1882 when they sold it to a young Irishman, J. A. Alcock, for $225,000.00.

Rhodes worked for them in 1885 when Jim Nabours, who appears in Emerson Hough's *North of 36*, was running the wagon. He worked for them again in the 1890s when Pete Johnson was running the wagon and the outfit claimed some 40,000 head on the Carrizozo Plain and southwards almost to Tularosa. Wm. C. McDonald, first state governor of New Mexico, was managing the syndicate at this time.

An account of this outfit's place in the cattle empire of A. B. Fall is given in Keleher's *The Fabulous Frontier*.

John Cross — Actually giving the J-Half Circle-Cross brand, this outfit was known as the John Cross to the exclusion of all other names.

With headquarters at Las Palomas, the John Cross ranged east of the river to the Black Range crest, between, roughly, Lake Valley and Cuchillo Negro. They claimed 40,000 head or more by 1888 and were the biggest outfit using Engle as shipping point and trading center.

The outfit was organized and promoted by Willard S. Hopewell with the money being provided by two Californians, William J. Borland and George W. Grayson, who had made it on the Comstock Lode during the days of Flood, Fair, O'Brien and Mackay.

The outfit overstocked their range and the drouth of 1890/1893 brought their decade of glory to a practical end. Most of their holdings are now owned by Tovrea Packing Company, Phoenix, Arizona.

K I M — Kim Ki Rogers' brand, started about 1883 on the *Jornada* and in the foothills of the Caballo Range, southwest of Engle. [See *Bar Cross*]

K Y — Brown & Hutchinson, Lexington, Kentucky, brought the first Durham cattle to the *Jornada*, at Aleman, about 1883. They had other holdings, apparently, on the San Augustin Plains or in American Valley, west of Magdalena. They sold out to a Kansas City man, Fred L. Forsha, who, in turn, sold to the 7 T X.

Rhodes' first job for hire was with the KY, cleaning out Jack Martin's well which had caved in. He was in the KY vicinity when Abran Garcia and some *compadres* had a 24-hour gun fight with the owners, shooting Perry Hutchinson "around the edges" but without serious casualities to either side.

Ladder — Started in the early 90s by Tom Ross, then wagon boss for the John Cross. Ranging between Hillsboro and Lake Valley, they came to run some 5,000 head before Ross sold out to Willard S. Hopewell about 1912. The properties are now owned by Tovrea Packing Co., Phoenix, Arizona.

7 T X — Known as "the Grant outfit" from its use of the Armendariz Grant, some 6 townships, running from just below Engle, northwards along the *Jornada* to San Marcial. Never fenced properly during Rhodes' days in that Country.

The Grant bought 600 yearling heifers in Texas in the T X brand, and ran the 7 on the shoulder for a tally brand, thus making the 7 T X on the *Jornada*. It and the Bar Cross were the two big outfits on the *Jornada* range proper.

Bob Martin took the wagon in 1894 and ran it for many years. The property was acquired by the Diamond A, called by Rhodes *The Broad A*, and still is owned by them so far as is known. Both 7 T X and Diamond A headquartered at Engle.

S S Bar — East of the Rio Grande on Cuchillo Creek and Willow Spring canyon. Owned by R. M. Snyder of Kansas City. Henry K. Street was their first wagon boss and Jack Chandler took over when he left. The outfit shipped and traded at Engle.

V Cross T — One of the biggest Free Range outfits in New Mexico and still operating so far as is known. In Rhodes' time, they shipped and traded at Magdalena covering most of the San Augustin Plains west of there to their headquarters on Beaver Canyon, under Black Mountain mesa in the Mogollons.

Cole Railston ran the wagon for several years after he left the Bar Cross.

LAGNIAPPE!

Gene Rhodes was a wordsmith; a lover of language; a master at the phrase-turning lathe. The selections which follow are those that have appealed to the bibliographer.

"She was wild and sweet and witty. Let's not say dull things about her."

"Nothing is so odd as a nudist in an overcoat."

"My brother writes me regularly every five years. But I do not answer promptly."

91

"Regards to all and sundried."

"Married men make the Worst husbands."

"I am the author of Cross Your Eyes and Damn Your Tees — a golfing story."

"A Bird in the Bush is the noblest work of God."

"Personally, I think the movies are nix and no credit to their sources. Too much of the old hokum bucket."

"In the seventeenth day of the twelfth month of my second childhood."

"Oh well! Maybe the next world will be most as good as this."

"Up with the lark or birds to that effect."

"I stood on a flush at midnight."

"I am unwilling to share my earned enemies."

"I have no objections to a dictator — except that he must do exactly as I wish. Otherwise, I revolt."

"A girl with two good men to choose from would deplore monogamy as a mistake."

"He had a wholesome sense of humor that went far to soften and ameliorate his many virtues."

"You cannot read my handwriting and I am not strong enough to use the typewriter — which makes each hair, even in health, stand on end like feathers on the fretful concubine."

"A *loyal* enemy will not tell any lies about you he doesn't believe himself."

"We asked for bread and they have given us a stein." [*On the repeal of Pro hibition during the Depression*]

PASO POR AQUI

There seems no better way to bring this compilation to a close than with the phrase that marks the great grave-boulder above Gene Rhodes last resting place high in the San Andrés Range where he brought in the bright mornings of his youth. It is used here as it first was used in print about Rhodes by Eugene Cunningham — without the accents so that it reads in present tense. As Rosalio Marquez, called "Monte" from his profession, said: *"Con razón* — eet ees weeth reason to do thees."

After the critics, the reviewers, the publishers — all things literary — have said their say and had their way, there remains the deep-rooted, unspoken, often unrecognized bond between author and reader that keeps that author alive, depite the verdicts of critics, reviewers, publishers — all things literary.

There has been scarcely a week during the last twelve years that a letter has not come my way bearing true witness that 'Gene Rhodes still lives. The excerpts that here are used have been selected by the one criterion of how nearly they meet Bernard DeVoto's statement about himself in his Foreword to *Mark Twain's America:* "My claim to some measure of authority in these pages derives from the fact that I have lived in a frontier community and known frontiersmen, as none of the literary folk who now exhibit ideas about frontier life have done. . . ."

The words hereafter were written by men and women who had lived in frontier communities and known frontiersmen.

From a mining man who knew my Father, dated November 26, 1946:

"My introduction to Rhodes may interest you. It was back in 1917 and I was in Phoenix, Arizona, on my honeymoon. Needless to say from what follows that I was first a settled bachelor and second a desert rat of long standing.

"It was before the days of cotton, niggers and poverty and in Phoenix men sat in hotel lobbies wearing Stetsons and high heel boots and the talk was of mining, cattle and women in the order named.

"Scouting through the one book store I found and which was really a notion shop, I ran across a copy of WEST IS WEST in the edition published by Fly.

"I have always been a sucker for a well-told, western yarn and the story opening in "El Paso del Norte" caught my eye. I sat up until 2:00 a. m. reading the book while my bride tossed and dozed.

"I need hardly say that I was not in good favor with the lady that day."

Back in the middle-Twenties, Aubrey Gist was running goats out of the old J K headquarters ranch on the Big Sandy southeast of Kingman, Arizona. Gist was then in middle-life and his trail reached eastwards behind him, across Arizona and New Mexico, where he had known Rhodes, to his Texas birthplace. We used to camp at Gist's trailing down off the high country under Mahon Mountain on our way to ship at Hackberry. Gist was a goatman and a *Tejano* to-boot, as noted, but he was a better neighbor, better man, than many of the local cow persons in that country. Early in 1947, one of his daughters wrote me a long letter about Rhodes from which the following is taken:

"Rhodes' work is already classic; I only hope that it can become more widely appreciated. Whether its honest authenticity, its perceptive delicacy can be gauged by later generations, I do not know. The yard-stick of comparison will perhaps have vanished with our own generation. For us, his people were the people we knew; the people who figured (for me) in my parent's reminiscent yarns. But they are going fast; how can a later generation savor their merit?"

From a Louisiana-born lady who went West came this comment in 1952:

"His entire output is the best record, best written, of a time and people almost departed. I have known his characters, under other names, in New Mexico,

West Texas, Arizona and Colorado. Like his pen and ink originals, they, too, have about disappeared. They made one of America's most colorful and interesting periods — probably the only purely native one — and the smoke into which they have evaporated is fragrant with their lives and deeds. 'Gene, himself, was the most colorful of them all."

At Christmas Season, 1946, this letter:

"The country north of Winnemucca [Nev.] is quite a bit west of my old stamping ground. I know a little of the country around Tuscarora and Mountain City. Once worked in a placer mine near the latter place. But my good days were spent between Wells, in Elko County, north to what we called the Snake River desert in Idaho. No one dreamed of the city of Twin Falls or the great irrigation developments around it.

"But that was a long time ago. I was just figuring. Forty-five years ago last October, my outfit — the Shoesole, Sparks-Harrell Cattle Co. — was camped on Shoshone Creek just north of the Idaho line. The heavy work was over. The first snow storm had cleared. I saddled up and told the boss I was going south and would see him next May when the spring roundup started from Rock Creek, Idaho. It was a promise I expected to keep but things did not break that way and it was not many springs before I found myself tied to a desk in Los Angeles — and with a growing family.

"Just before the last war [*II*] I did what I had threatened to do for many years. I took my car and drove up to the old range. I came back depressed; you cannot backtrack in life. It wasn't the absence of the saddled horses standing at the hitching racks on the ranches. Or the blocky whitefaces that can't run fast enough to get out of their own way. It was the absence of something intangible but very real. I think it was the absence of a feeling of remoteness and everything that remoteness and isolation do to men.

"I talked with two or three riders. They were good hands; could ride and knew their work. But these boys had felt the full impact of the outside world. They knew what Greta Garbo wore and had heard the King of England speak over the radio. It was different in the old days. I knew fellows who had no contact with the outside world except when we shipped beef at Tecoma, Nevada. Or perhaps a stray newspaper, or, rarely, a passing stranger. And if you cut the track of a strange rider you generally followed it up far enough to decide whether he was passing through or not.

"Well, it's no use growing maudlin over old times. The march of time is inexorable and in the American West very fast. But riding is still a good job. A horse is still a horse and you can see a long way yet in Nevada. If you have never known anything different you probably don't mind the long ribbons of asphalt. Or even the government man breathing down the back of your neck and telling you when and where you can run your stock and charging you rent for the open range.

"Well, here's hoping you succeed in keeping the honest atmosphere of Rhodes' works from being entirely submerged by the flood of synthetic 'western.'"

The comments of Joe De Yong, taken from letters of March and April, 1956, are worth reading;

"I grew up in the Cherokee Nation and in the normal course of events became a kid-cowpuncher; a life that, under ordinary circumstances, I would undoubtedly have followed for the rest of my days. However, I lost my hearing and all sense of balance as the result of a serious illness shortly before my nineteenth birthday. As a result — and even though I immediately had a short-treed saddle made, and learned to ride again, my cowpunching days were over. (Due to pride, more than anything else!)

"In any case, I was a born reader and had already become inoculated with Rhodes particular form of magic; due, mostly, to the fact that his stories, his plots, his characters, reflected the same sort of thinking that I had become accustomed to looking for in my own surroundings. Another point that tripled his range was, that he instinctively knew — inside, outside and on the darkest night — the *great* difference between a Cowpuncher and a *Cowman!*"

Finally, these excerpts from a letter written on May 2, 1958:

"A Western folklore is in the making and I hope it will be founded on truth and have the old Western flavor, the whimsy and dry philosophy of the old Westerners. If it is to be based on the present day writers for the screen and television, it is going to be as flat as cooking without salt.

"If committing the perfect crime is a feat, the production of a 'perfect' Western without personal knowledge and depending upon research and imagination only is a greater one. There are few authors who wrote of the West from real personal knowledge. Rhodes is the only one I know of who could perform the acts his characters executed. The life in the old West demanded a number of skills which were not easy to learn. Rhodes had them.

"It is important to preserve Rhodes' work for the two reasons given in the two paragraphs above.

"When I read one of his stories, I feel the dark blue sky, the warm sun reflected from an adobe wall, hear the pungent talk of cow men squatting on their heels, their tall tales of the '80s, Rhodes' own characters come to life. I can confirm his own words. His tales were authentic.

"Don't get the impression I am a professional Westerner. If you ran into me without any knowledge of my life, you would be puzzled. But I am human, drifting and faraway. Home always calls and when I read about Rhodes' New Mexico I feel a tug some where down deep."

A good many days out of one man's life have been poured into amassing the details that have made this book. It may seem to many to have been an unnecessary labor or an overweening obsession. *Quien Sabe?* 'Gene Rhodes played an integral, even a vital part in the development of the "Western" which, with *le jazz Hot,* makes the finest native flowering of our culture. For this reason, then, my personal feelings after twelve years of laboring in the vineyard can best be expressed in some words Rhodes gave to a friend of his:

"Why, one time I drew to the six and eight of diamonds and made an ace full! Man, it was just shameful!"

SON TODOS

REFERENCE ROOM

JUN 14 1968